Entrepreneur. Press

MASTERING ONLINE MARKETING

MITCH MEYERSON
FOUNDER OF GUERRILLA MARKETING COACHING
WITH MARY EULE SCARBOROUGH

Jere L. Calmes, publisher
Front cover design: Erin N. Calmes
Back cover design: Beth Hansen-Winter
Composition and production: MillerWorks

This publication is designed to provide accurate and authoritative information in regard to the subject matter covered. It is sold with the understanding that the publisher is not engaged in rendering legal, accounting, or other professional services. If legal advice or other expert assistance is required, the services of a competent professional person should be sought.

Library of Congress Cataloging-in-Publication Data

Meyerson, Mitch.
    Mastering online marketing / by Mitch Meyerson and Mary Eule Scarborough.
        p. cm.
    ISBN-13: 978-1-59918-151-6 (alk. paper)
    ISBN-10: 1-59918-151-7 (alk. paper)
        1. Internet marketing. 2. Internet advertising. 3. Electronic commerce–Marketing.
        I. Scarborough, Mary Eule. II. Title.
HF5415.1265.M467 2007   658.8'72–dc22
2007021488

Printed in Canada

12 11 10 09   10 9 8 7 6 5 4 3

CONTENTS

CHAPTER 4
DESIGN AND NAVIGATION:
MAKING YOUR WEB SITE DYNAMIC AND VISITOR-FRIENDLY 69

CHAPTER 5
DYNAMIC WEB COPY: THE KEY TO GETTING PEOPLE TO RESPOND 93

CHAPTER 10
PEOPLE POWER:
THE KEY TO SUCCESSFUL AFFILIATE PROGRAMS AND PARTNERSHIPS 205

CHAPTER 11
WEB 2.0: THE KEY TO USING SOCIAL MEDIA EFFECTIVELY 221

CHAPTER 12
MOMENTUM: THE KEY TO SYSTEMATIZING YOUR BUSINESS AND
BUILDING YOUR VIRTUAL TEAM

Not long ago, I was a well-known and respected psychotherapist living and working in Chicago, one of the most vibrant cities in the world. I had studied many years to earn my degree, and I was working hard every day to grow my practice. I even managed to eke out enough time to co-author three psychology books. I felt fortunate to have a successful practice, a nice home, a comfortable lifestyle, good friends, and a beautiful downtown office. Yet I wasn't happy.

You see, as anyone who has lived in the northern Midwest knows, the winters can be incredibly cold, awfully gray, and very, very long. And when I say cold, I mean *really* cold. That bone-chilling, feet-numbing, teeth-chattering, purple-fingers kind of cold.

But the worst part about it for me was the gray sky. There were times when the sun disappeared for what felt like months.

During these times, I imagined what it would be like to live and work in a warmer climate with blue skies and sunshine. You know... the kind of place where you can play tennis and swim every day of the year if you want. I imagined having time to fulfill my creative dream of writing and recording music... time to experience real community with my close friends... time to really live and enjoy every day. But after I basked in my dream for a while, I was always jolted back to reality. Sure, I could have moved, but the thought of starting from scratch, in a new location, giving up the steady income I'd grown accustomed to, felt daunting.

THE BREAKTHROUGH MOMENT

Looking for an answer, I spent more time on the internet and noticed that there was an emerging group of coaches, counselors, and trainers starting to build virtual businesses (meaning they were conducted over the phone and internet). I immediately realized that this was an incredible opportunity for me to create a business and lifestyle that defied geographic boundaries.

I began studying the web sites and programs of the most successful online entrepreneurs, and over time I became convinced that I could learn from them and connect with people all over the world. This would enable me to do what I loved and create streams of income using the internet. I came to know, deep down, that my dream could be a reality. I decided to go for it.

In less than three years, I was earning more than enough income to leave Chicago and move to the clear blue skies of Scottsdale, Arizona, where I live today. My first breakthrough program was a joint venture with Jay Levinson, the father of Guerrilla Marketing. Combining my expertise in coaching and program development with his marketing model, I created the Guerrilla Marketing Coaching Program. There I trained small-business owners to market their companies using low-cost, high-impact strategies and helped others become Certified Guerrilla Marketing Coaches. I marketed and delivered the program over the phone and internet, through teleseminars supported by a web site and downloadable curriculum materials.

Since then I've worked hard to improve my skills, and as a result I am now delivering a more robust and higher-quality version of my original program and have substantially expanded my product and service offerings as well. My success with the Guerrilla Marketing Coaching Program attracted another excellent partner, Michael Port, with whom I created the 90-Day Product Factory and the Traffic School. These courses, and my subsequent offerings, have attracted clients from all over the world.

LIVING THE DREAM

Now I swim in my waterfall pool daily, bask in the sunshine, play tennis often, write and produce the music I love, relax in my hot tub, enjoy time with my closest friends, and run my thriving e-commerce business from the comfort of my home. I am happy to say I am truly living my dream.

I could never have accomplished this, however, without a clear vision, effective partnerships, and the ability to market successfully over the internet.

Whatever the vision for your ideal life is, I am confident that the insights found in the pages of this book will help lead you there.

May you create the life you desire,

Mitch Meyerson

Scottsdale, AZ

www.MitchMeyerson.com

I love brilliant people. I love the way their minds work. I love the adventure they take me on. I love to wrestle with them, to be challenged by them, to engage in dialogue with them. I love to listen to their words, and to follow them where they take me.

Mitch Meyerson is such a person. It's obvious that he's comfortable playing big games and has a knack for helping others to play them as well.

Much like *The E-Myth*, *Mastering Online Marketing* is not just a collection of tools and tactics. Mitch has created a solid step-by step system for you to build and sustain a thriving e-commerce business. He describes the things that will trip you up, the things that will liberate you, the things you must never do, and the things you absolutely, so help you God, must do if you want to become a kick-ass online marketer.

But perhaps the thing I love most about this book is its profound clarity. Mitch and his partner, Mary Eule Scarborough, have done an outstanding job of presenting complex information in a clear and concise, yet thorough, manner.

Many of us want to rise above ourselves. And even though we have the desire to achieve our goals we sometimes falter as we take the first few steps. Often this is simply because we do not have the power to see things clearly. We're not sure what steps to take first, second, third and so on. This book will show you the way. Read it. Digest it. Follow it letter by letter. Then get out there and *do it*—because that's how you'll experience the true rewards.

And then let Mitch and me know how you did. Because success stories are what we love the best.

Michael E. Gerber
Author of *The E-Myth* books

ACKNOWLEDGMENTS

Special thanks to Mary Eule Scarborough for her insights, dedication, and brilliant writing on this book. Thank you also to:

- Michael Port and Jay Conrad Levinson for partnering with me to create amazing programs over the internet.

- Jere Calmes for believing in this book from the beginning.

- Amy Belanger, David Scarborough, and Peggy Murrah for their wonderful contributions.

And finally to all the Certified Guerrilla Marketing Coaches and students in my online programs for their entrepreneurial spirit and for taking the virtual road less traveled. What a ride.

THE ENTREPRENEURIAL SHIFT

The Key to Creating an Integrated Business Mindset

In this chapter you'll learn

- *the good news: why it's a great time to build an e-commerce web site*

- *tips for overcoming four universal success blockers*

- *personality traits of winners*

- *how to develop your own vision by beginning at the end*

...and much more.

" Most entrepreneurs are merely technicians...

with an entrepreneurial seizure. Most entrepreneurs fail because you are working *in* your business rather than *on* your business."

—*Michael Gerber, author of* The E-Myth

Want to start an online business? Perhaps you'd like to

- drive traffic to your brick-and-mortar retail location
- write an e-book on ways to improve a golf swing
- sell your own, or others', products
- acquire new clients for your consulting business
- connect with other like-minded people
- obtain new subscribers for your mailing list
- sell supplemental products or services to existing customers
- educate people on a particular subject
- generate more awareness about your company's products or services.

Great idea! There's never been a better time to take advantage of the expansive opportunities for online business development and growth that the internet affords. But there's more to building a thriving online business than getting your site up. There are some very important things you need to know first. So sit down, grab your favorite drink, and get ready to read and learn.

THE IMPORTANCE OF LEARNING SOLID BUSINESS STRATEGIES

While online businesses are unique in many ways, your e-commerce site is merely a tool that you will use to help you achieve your personal and professional goals.

Therefore, you should develop yours using the same sound, time-tested, and well-thought-out business methodologies that companies have used for generations. Yes, the internet is relatively new, but good business skills have been around for thousands of years.

The purpose of this book is to take you by the hand and teach you easy-to-understand strategies and tactics for building your own booming online business. And since this action guide is a follow-up to my previous book *Success Secrets of the Online Marketing Superstars*, I'll share more details, advice, and tips from the world's most respected online marketing superstars—the select few who have a proven track record of creating and sustaining wildly profitable e-commerce web sites.

If you pay close attention and use these valuable strategies and tactics, you will substantially increase the odds of creating your own successful online business. And over time the mindset, methodologies, and concepts I'll introduce to you will become second nature—just like muscle memory.

THE FOUR STAGES OF LEARNING

One of the most useful models I've used to explain the learning process is often referred to as the Four Stages of Learning. The stages are:

1. **Unconscious Incompetence.** Said another way, "We don't know what we don't know." A simple example of this is a baffled tennis player who continually puts the ball into the net when he hits his backhand shot. He doesn't know why it's happening and may not even know how to find out. In other words, he doesn't know what his problem is and doesn't know how to identify it, let alone fix it. Ironically, however, he feels completely confident that the ball will soon sail over the net easily even if he does nothing to change his swing. Have you ever heard the expression "Ignorance is bliss"?

2. **Conscious Incompetence.** During this second stage, we know what we don't know. We realize that our skill in a particular area is limited and we need help in order to improve. For example, this is when our frustrated tennis player hires an instructor to help him improve his grip and correct his backhand swing. Although he could reasonably expect to hit fewer balls into the net, his results will still be very inconsistent. Getting through this phase can be daunting because inconsistency may feel more like failure.

3. **Conscious Competence.** In this learning phase, we have the skills, know-how, and ability to complete the task proficiently, but we still must concentrate carefully. We know what we know, but we have to think about it. During this stage, our tennis player continues to practice his backhand shot and works hard to use the right grip and swing the racket correctly. His confidence grows as the ball gets over the net more often than not.

4. **Unconscious competence.** This is the stage when it all comes together. We can perform the given task successfully, even when we have other things on our minds. Our tennis player is now a backhand champ and gets the ball over the net even when he's thinking about what he's having for lunch!

What does this have to do with online marketing? Everything. In order to build a strong e-commerce business, you'll need to learn new skills, obtain vital information, adopt a winning attitude, and use the tools and methodologies I outline in this book. And if you devote the time, practice, and patience it requires—regardless of which learning phase you're in now—you'll stand a far greater chance of succeeding, than if you do not.

THE GOOD NEWS

These are amazing times for online entrepreneurs! It's never been easier to transform a local brick-and-mortar company into a thriving business that serves clients worldwide from the comfort of your home. Now prospects from every continent can visit your virtual store, opt in, and securely purchase your products or services in a matter of minutes! And because of many factors, the appeal of owning your own e-commerce business is even more enticing. That's why people from every walk of life—Fortune 500 executives, service professionals, stay-at-home moms, packaged goods retailers, freelance writers, and so on—are searching for a better way and jumping on the internet bandwagon.

Perhaps they imagine a life where commuting and dark suits are things of the past, or one where they no longer have to worry about layoffs and downsizing, or that allows them to spend more time with their family, or where they can conduct business while sipping mango smoothies on a sunny beach in Tahiti. And it's never been easier to turn these dreams into realities. Easy-to-use, state-of-the-art computer software and technology provide *everyone* the opportunity to alter the way they work, improve their lifestyle, and achieve their loftiest ambitions. Consider this:

■ According to a Juniper Research study, the number of U.S. internet shoppers will grow at an average rate of 12 percent per year through 2010, resulting in more than $144 billion in online sales.

- Additionally, experts predict that by 2010, 50 percent of traditional and e-commerce purchases will be substantially impacted by research conducted by consumers online, indicating that all retailers need to develop multiple sales channels and fully assimilate their online and offline strategies.

- Over the next several years, online retail growth will be driven not only by an increase in the number of consumers but also by a boost in the average spending amount per buyer—predicted to be nearly $780 per year, per consumer, by 2008. Until now the tremendous growth of online businesses has been driven by the steady increase in new online shoppers.

These positive forecasts should be music to the ears of any aspiring e-commerce entrepreneur.

THE OTHER SIDE OF THE STORY

As growth increases, competition will heat up as well. Online merchants—those who have established a solid and trusted track record—will find it far easier to compete for new and existing online shoppers. Others will not. It's my job to see that your business in among those in the first group.

Since I am entirely invested in your e-commerce success, I'm not going to pull any punches. So, in addition to heartily supporting your online business goals and providing you with valuable tools, tips, and strategies, I must also be candid and discuss some hard truths. In order to get this right, let's talk about the elephant in the room.

WHY MOST ONLINE BUSINESSES FAIL

Entrepreneurs drive the U.S. economy. They have the fervor, oomph, tenacity, and spirit to achieve remarkable prosperity and independence. Far more action oriented than others, they make things happen rather than wait for things to happen to them. Unfortunately, their behavior pattern is a double-edged sword.

Many online marketers mistakenly leap into action and rush to build their web sites—without giving the process sufficient time, thought, and planning—enticed by the gobs of money they'll earn and the relatively low cost

> ## "There's an elephant in the room...
>
> so it is hard to get around it. Yet we squeeze by with "How are you?" and "I'm fine!" and a thousand other forms of trivial chatter. We talk about the weather. We talk about work. We talk about everything else... except the elephant in the room. We all know it is there."
>
> —*Terry Kettering,* The Elephant in the Room

of entry. They falsely believe that they can create a profitable business even though they lack the vital information and tools necessary to carry them through successfully.

And although most of them are smart, passionate, hardworking, and innovative people—ones who share dreams similar to your own—they nevertheless learn, and ultimately live, a hard and often unspoken truth: *the majority of online businesses fail.*

So why do so many e-commerce businesses fail? And what can you do to ensure that yours thrives? The obvious answer to the first question is that companies cease to exist for a multitude of reasons. Despite common lore, businesses seldom go under because of one shattering event (even though one is often cited as the official cause). Rather, online businesses (and all others) go bust because *lots of mistakes, most seemingly small, were made over an extended period of time.*

Here's a simple analogy that my friend and colleague David A. Scarborough, a former Air Force aviator and private flight instructor, uses: A pilot wants to fly from New York to San Francisco in five hours. His flight plan directs him to maintain a westerly heading of 260 degrees. If he sustains this exact compass direction during the entire flight, he will reach his destination... that is, unless he encounters a simple northerly wind, which will surely blow him off course.

In this case the pilot must alter his compass heading (e.g., 270 degrees instead of 260 degrees) to offset the effects of the wind and stay on course. And if he doesn't continually make small adjustments to his settings (to compensate for external factors) throughout the entire flight, he will not reach his intended destination.

Lucky for today's aviators, state-of-the-art aircraft are equipped with automatic pilots that continually correct the plane's direction many times per second, making it unnecessary for pilots to correct them manually. As a budding online entrepreneur you must learn to do the same: continually adjust for the changing winds of the business environment. You must also compensate for your own internal *success blockers*—those attitudes, ideas, and skill limits that are standing in your way. Like the pilot, there are many variables that can get a business off course, but if they are corrected, it will survive.

I stress this because I've personally worked with hundreds of small business owners who did not pay attention to their own success blockers. Like the elephant in the room, your seemingly minor miscalculations may be easier and more comfortable—at least initially—to ignore than to face. But if you're really serious about building and maintaining a profitable e-commerce business you should begin by reading the following list of the five most common business roadblocks. Although this is a complex subject—the topic of many lengthy books—consider which ones, if any, describe your own attitudes and behaviors. Once you've identified them, implement an improvement plan.

BUSINESS ROADBLOCK #1: Believing That Being a Good Craftsman Is All That's Needed to Run a Successful Business

Many folks erroneously believe that being an exceptional craftsman (e.g., financial advisor, quilter, therapist, fundraiser, speaker, etc.) makes them qualified to operate a business that specializes in that work. They spend most of their time performing the work of the business rather than leading, planning, organizing, systematizing, and/or marketing their company!

Most of us know people like these: They must be at work

> ## Entrepreneurship is like camping.
> You're complaining the whole time, but when you look back at it, you think, 'That was pretty neat.'"
> —*Jim Steiner, businessman*

every day in order to conduct their business. They do it all: pack boxes, write invoices, make sales calls, answer the phone, fix equipment, design their own web site, write their own ad copy, trouble-shoot problems, empty the trash,

meet personally with every client, and so on. They have no written procedures, documented processes, or automated systems for doing anything.
Rather, their valuable knowledge, innovative ideas, and sound methodologies
remain only in their heads.

You also won't find them outsourcing work, forming beneficial strategic
alliances, delegating tasks to employees, or seeking wise counsel from other
professionals. Why? Because many entrepreneurs believe they already know what they need to know—and they don't want to know what they don't know! Like the hapless and overconfident tennis player we met earlier, they are unconsciously incompetent and if they remain that way, their business will most certainly fail.

> ## "If they don't fail outright,
> most businesses fail to fully achieve their potential. That's because the person who owns the business doesn't truly know how to build a company that works without him or her… which is the key."
>
> —*Michael Gerber, author of* The E-Myth

So what happens? They try to go
it alone. They get sick. They get sick and tired. They get stretched too thin.
They feel rushed and overwhelmed. They worry that they can't do it all. They
worry that others won't do it right. They know that they should let go but
can't. They worry about what it might cost them to let go. They fail to fix serious flaws. They ignore their customers. They have a short-term, "put-out-the-
latest-fire" mentality. They feel like they need to get away. They take a
much-needed vacation and when they return they discover that their business has come to a screeching halt. The work has piled up and they've lost
money, frustrated customers, and missed golden opportunities.

Tips for Staying on Course

- **Realize that being good at something does not mean you'll succeed at running a business that does that work.**
- **Objectively assess your business skills and knowledge.** Begin by taking the Business Mindset Self-Assessment Test included in this chapter (see
  page 19). Answer the questions honestly so you can identify your business

strengths and weaknesses. (Please note: If, after taking the self-assessment, you're convinced that you're the right person for every job, retake the test.)

- **Play to your strengths, passions, and skills.** Do what you do best and let others help you. Build a team of people—employees, consultants, strategic partners, and the like—who are more skilled than you in key areas.

- **Seek support from others outside of work—family, friends and colleagues—and offer support as well.** Make sure to take advantage of the vast resources available on the internet.

- **Automate!** With all of the affordable technology available today—software, phone systems, web-based programs—there's no excuse for going it alone. It's never been easier to communicate with prospects, troubleshoot problems, and stay in contact with customers and the like, from wherever you happen to be.

BUSINESS ROADBLOCK #2: Lack of Clearly Articulated Goals

Did you know that the very act of identifying and writing down your goals substantially increases your chances of becoming successful? If so, you may be surprised to learn that (in my experience), most entrepreneurs do not articulate their goals, define the action steps required to achieve a given goal, or track and measure their progress.

Tips for Staying on Course

- **Identify your lifestyle goals.** What do you really want? More money? More time with your family? More freedom?

- **Visualize.** Once you've developed your goals, it's time to expand to your online business vision. Think about what you want to achieve in the long and short term. Make sure your objectives support your lifestyle ambitions.

- **Develop a plan.** It's time to work on the "SMART" techniques you'll use to achieve your overall vision. Is your action plan Specific, Measurable, Actionable, Realistic, and Time-Based? If not, it's back to the drawing board.

- **Prioritize.** Decide which elements must be included, amended, or erased. But remain flexible and revisit them often, because things change.

- **Break down the plan.** Divide your action steps into smaller chunks, and eat that elephant one bite at a time!

A To-Do List for Life

Legendary author and marketing expert Mark Victor Hansen has sold more than 100 million books and products in the last ten years alone. When it comes to thinking big and implementing aggressive plans, he is a master. Mark's latest book series, which he co-authored with Robert Allen, is *The One Minute Millionaire* and their goal is to inspire one million new millionaires this decade.

The following excerpt is from *Success Secrets of the Online Marketing Superstars.*

Before we set off on this path together, let me make one thing very clear: The word "goals" can be intimidating—it can feel so overbearing that it keeps people from even beginning the process. So, let's instead think of goals as a "To-Do List with Deadlines." Do the deadlines have to be tomorrow? Next week? Of course not. This is your To-Do List for the rest of your life. Goals can be added to, subtracted from, and most importantly—scratched off the list as you move through your life. Here's a checklist to ensure you're using a successful framework to set your To-Do List:

- **Your most important goals must be yours.** Not your spouse's. Not your child's. Not your employer's. Yours. When you let other people determine your definition of success, you're sabotaging your own future.

- **Your goals must mean something to you.** When you write your goals, you must ask yourself, "What's really important to me?" "What am I prepared to give up to make this happen?" Your reasons for charting a new course of action give you the drive and energy to get up every morning.

- **Your goals must be specific and measurable.** Vague generalizations and wishy-washy statements aren't good enough. Be very specific!

- **Your goals must be flexible.** A flexible plan keeps you from feeling suffocated and allows you to take advantage of genuine opportunities that may walk in your door.

- **Your goals must be challenging and exciting.** Force yourself to jump out of your comfort zone to acquire that energy and edge.

- **Your goals must be in alignment with your values.** Pay attention to your intuition—your gut. When you set a goal that contradicts your values, something inside will twinge. Pay attention.

- **Your goals must be well balanced.** Make sure you include areas that allow time to relax, have fun and enjoy people in your closest circle.

- **Your goals must be realistic.** Be expansive but don't be ridiculous. If you're four feet tall, you will probably never play in the NBA. Also, be sure to allow yourself time to get there.

- **Your goals must include contribution.** Unfortunately, many people get so wrapped up in pursuing their day-to-day lives that they don't have time to give something back to society. Build this into your goals program.

- **Your goals need to be supported.** Either selectively share a few of your dreams with a number of people, or share all of your dreams with a select few people. In either case, you're creating a web of support and accountability for yourself.

Open your mind to all the possibilities. Start each goal with "I am" or "I will." Don't even think about restricting yourself!

(Used with permission. *Success Secrets of the Online Marketing Superstars*, Kaplan Publishing, formerly Dearborn.)

BUSINESS ROADBLOCK #3: Lack of Focus, Distraction, and Overcommitment

Folks with this roadblock often describe themselves as idea people (which is another way of saying that you're likely to find them wandering aimlessly from one thing to another, never sure of what to do next). They tend to juggle multiple projects at once, start things they don't finish, say yes to any request, and appear to be constantly distracted.

So what happens? You guessed it: they become bored, exhausted, overwhelmed, confused, and frustrated, and lack the energy to do what is most important. Thus, their real priorities—those tasks that result in the biggest benefits—get lost in the shuffle and ultimately forgotten and dropped.

What else happens? They procrastinate! Most of us have been guilty of putting off things that need to be completed. However, for some, procrastinating is a way of life. They are usually running around with their hair on fire, always in "urgent" mode. They do things sloppily, late, or not at all; look for short-term bandages instead of long-term cures; and commit avoidable blunders and waste precious time on costly rework. If this sounds like you, it is imperative that you uncover the root causes of your procrastination and work on overcoming it right away, because leaving it unchecked will make it nearly impossible to create a profitable on-line business.

Tips for Staying on Course

- **Prioritize.** Create a daily to-do list each evening and number your tasks according to their importance. Then make sure you complete the most important one *first*, before moving onto the next.
- **Master your calendar.** You are in control of your own time, so learn to become a careful scheduler, even if it means you have to make appointments with yourself for lunch.
- **Slow down.** Rome wasn't built in a day and your business won't be either.
- **Learn to say no.** Realize that when you take on something, you usually have to give up something else. Drop time-consuming and unnecessary

jobs and delegate more. Unloading your schedule will significantly decrease stress, increase your ability to focus, and result in accomplishing far more!

BUSINESS ROADBLOCK #4: Conflicting Intentions

Have you ever heard someone referred to as his or her own worst enemy? Do you wonder why many of us often seem to interfere with our own success? If so, you probably recognize that in spite of our constructive intentions to do something—become a successful online marketer, lose weight, call a relative, get that promotion—we don't always follow through.

And in many instances it is not a simple case of procrastination. Rather, it is more insidious, an often unconscious choice to achieve two opposing goals—ones that essentially make it impossible to accomplish either, because they cancel each other out.

Conflicting intentions are equal-opportunity blockers, and they come in every imaginable form. During my many years of consulting with entrepreneurs, I've seen them all. Here are just a few:

"I want to earn six figures next year working two hours per week."

"I'm working hard to get rich even though my gut tells me that's a selfish goal."

"I'm trying to increase my business, but I'm not sure I'm ready to take on more customers."

"I want to be successful, but I don't want to do things that I don't like."

So what happens? These folks feel trapped and confused. Their dreams seem futile and their results are second-rate at best.

Tips for Staying on Course

First, acknowledge that you have conflicting intentions even though they're usually far more emotional than logical and may be buried deep in your subconscious. Then try this:

1. Make yourself a promise and write it down. For example, "I promise that I will spend one hour five times per week reading a good book."

2. Underneath your promise, list all of the things that can stand in the way of you keeping your pledge. For example:

I have to work late most nights so won't have time.

I have too many important responsibilities that should take precedence.

It's an hour I won't spend with my spouse.

Now, go back to the list you made in step 2 and write down your supporting belief for each roadblock. For example, under "It's an hour I won't spend with my spouse," you might put, "I'll be perceived as selfish and uncaring." If you dig even further, you might come up with "If I don't pay attention to my family, they'll stop loving me." Once you've identified these beliefs, you can begin challenging their veracity and making positive changes.

Working at Cross Purposes

Steps 1 and 2 actually represent your conflicting intentions. Step 1 is encouraging you to act differently—to change in a meaningful way. Conversely, the items you listed in Step 2 are convincing you that your promise is not worth the price you'll pay and urging you to let it go.

This type of internal assessment will be invaluable as you build and maintain your online business. Start by defining your own positive intentions—what you want to happen. Then ensure that you are willing to embrace the journey. Delve into your own conflicting intentions: face them, challenge them, and work hard to gain mastery over them.

BUSINESS ROADBLOCK #5: No Systematized Processes

One of the biggest mistakes entrepreneurs commit is failing to document, systematize, and communicate key processes (series of action steps), instructions, and information. They keep information in their head and rarely write it down. They try in vain to manage their employees, suppliers, and co-workers and often appear frustrated over their performance. For example, the outcome of any business task is dependent upon three things:

1. **Systems.** The overall structure, plan, and organization of tasks.

2. **Processes.** Detailed action items associated with accomplishing objectives, including the specific tasks, order of performance, timeline, and person(s) responsible for completing them.

3. **People.** Those who are accountable for completing the work.

When one, or more, of these pieces are overlooked, a business becomes vulnerable. So what happens? These people waste time. They get confused. They feel out of control. Solving problems is a nightmare. Training people to do anything is difficult and time-consuming. They don't measure results, because they don't know how.

Tips for Staying on Course

- **Manage processes, not people.** Focus less on handling people and more on providing clearly written processes for completing all key tasks. (I talk about this more in Chapter 12 and provide a template for documenting yours.) Then make sure that all tasks have owners who have the tools, information, and time necessary to complete the task successfully, and that the owners understand that they are accountable for finishing their tasks properly and on time.

- **Automate!** Take advantage of affordable, easy-to-use software to help you document and systematize your business processes. For example, if you routinely correspond with your customer base, as you should, use autoresponders (more about these in Chapter 7). They automatically send your prewritten correspondence on the dates you designate. Database and web systems can also be used for invoicing, payment confirmation, product delivery, and more.

- **Develop a simple, step-by-step system for completing tasks.** For example, if you produce a monthly e-zine, delegate the content development, editing, design, and release to others and establish a production schedule. I've provided a sample of how one might look in Figure 1-1.

Task	Person Responsible	Deadline	Notes
Content development	Mark	20th	Deliver to Jennifer by noon.
Editing	Jennifer	24th	Deliver to Carol by noon.
Design	Carol	27th	Deliver to Mitch by noon.
Approval	Mitch	29th	Deliver to Peggy by noon.
Release	Peggy	30th	Release by noon; send confirmation to team.

FIGURE 1-1. E-Zine Production Schedule

PERSONALITY TRAITS OF SUCCESSFUL BUSINESSPEOPLE

Thousands of pundits, experts, philosophers, and scientists have conducted research in an attempt to discover the common characteristics that successful people possess. And while opinions vary, most agree that those belonging to this elite group share the following ten personality traits. Look them over and see how you fare. Check your strengths and note areas where you may be weak. Not sure how you rate? Ask colleagues, family and friends to help you out. If you'd like to print out several copies of this list, visit www. OnlineMarketing Templates.com

TEN PERSONALITY TRAITS OF ACCOMPLISHED PEOPLE

They are:

1. **Conscientious and reliable.** They deliver on their promises.
2. **Altruistic and considerate.** They truly care about the welfare of others and demonstrate this concern often.
3. **Flexible.** They follow a plan but understand, expect, and even welcome change.
4. **Able to give and receive constructive feedback.** They have the courage to accept and provide specific feedback and constructive coaching.

5. **Passionate and enthusiastic.** They have the fervor, energy, and interest necessary to fuel their all-important vision.

6. **Optimistic**. They are positive thinkers who choose to see the best in people and situations but are not afraid to confront the cold, hard,

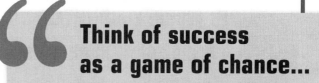

Think of success as a game of chance...

in which you have control over the odds. As you begin to master concepts in personal achievement, you are increasing your odds of achieving success."

—*Bo Bennett, author and businessman*

facts and weigh the risks in any new venture. They use their energy and resources to figure out ways to make things work, rather than think about why they won't.

7. **Committed to life-long learning.** They ask questions, search for knowledge and information, value education, and respect others who do so as well.

8. **Tenacious and persistent.** They don't give up when the going gets rough.

9. **Balanced in mind, body, and spirit.** They possess the mental, physical, and emotional intelligence and skills necessary to perform their job responsibilities at a high level.

10. **Focused on the long term.** They understand that part of the work they do today is building long-term relationships with employees, clients, and vendors, and planning for their future.

Three Success Factors

In the May 2005 issue of the *Monthly Labor Review* (volume 128, number 5), researcher and writer Amy E. Knaup weighed in on the three major factors that determine a company's chance of succeeding. They are:

1. Sufficient capital, especially as it relates to hiring employees and/or outsourcing work

2. The owner's education level and values

3. The founder's reason for starting the business in the first place (e.g., freedom, family life, passion)

WEB WORK: YOUR INTERACTIVE ADVENTURE

1. CALCULATE YOUR BUSINESS IQ

Now that you have a better understanding about the vital role your skills, interests, and personality play in the success of your online business, it's time to identify your own business strengths and weaknesses. To help you with this, I've developed a 30-item business self-assessment test. It is a great way to gain revealing insights into your business strengths and weaknesses, in 15 minutes or less (see Figure 1-2). If you answer each question honestly, and I sincerely hope you do, you'll discover what beliefs and/or behaviors will help you build and maintain a profitable online business as well as the ones that may be standing in your way.

After you've finished the quiz, add up your score and refer to the "Score Interpretation" section that follows to see how well you've done. Even if your score indicates that you would benefit from assistance from professionals such as a career coach, business consultant, financial planner, etc., that's OK— it's better to find that out sooner rather than later. Good luck!

Score Interpretation

If your total points equal 75 or less, your business mindset needs improvement. The good news, however, is that you have a wonderful opportunity to grow and learn, and it starts right here. Instead of settling for less than you'd like, use the strategies and tactics provided in this guide to realize the true potential of your online business. Also consider getting help from other professionals, such as a marketing coach, business consultant, financial advisor, or virtual assistant.

If your score is between 76 and 119, you've got a respectable business mindset, but there's always room for improvement. You could realistically expect to improve your overall online business performance by carefully following the strategies and tactics presented in this action book.

If your total points equal or exceed 120, good for you! You've got the right attitude and personality to achieve your online business goals. But now is not the time to rest. Take advantage of the strategies and tactics presented in this guide to make your e-commerce business soar!

FIGURE 1-2. Business Mindset Self-Assessment Test

Name: _____ Date: _____

Company: _____

Directions: Circle the appropriate number for each statement listed. Once completed, add up your scores. Then refer to the "Score Interpretation" section to see where you stand.

Please note: In order to improve accuracy, the statements are not grouped and or listed in any particular order.

	Strongly Disagree	Often Disagree	Sometimes Agree	Often Agree	Strongly Agree
1. I constantly seek out new information and use it to improve my business skills.	1	2	3	4	5
2. I know how to present ideas effectively (written, face-to-face, over the telephone).	1	2	3	4	5
3. I prioritize and maintain an effective schedule based on my time and resources available.	1	2	3	4	5
4. I use an effective decision-making process for all key business issues.	1	2	3	4	5
5. I often seek advice from business experts.	1	2	3	4	5
6. I know what the biggest challenges to my business are, and work to fix them.	1	2	3	4	5
7. I have written systems and processes in place that allow me to delegate some of the day-to-day duties.	1	2	3	4	5
8. I take responsibility for my decisions.	1	2	3	4	5
9. I am passionate about my business and can't think of anything else I'd rather do.	1	2	3	4	5
10. I have a written business and marketing plan.	1	2	3	4	5
11. I am committed to becoming a student of business and marketing.	1	2	3	4	5
12. I know my greatest strengths and weaknesses.	1	2	3	4	5
13. I am committed to investing time, effort, and focus to learning better ways to improve sales, profits, and performance.	1	2	3	4	5
14. I actively seek out strategic partners.	1	2	3	4	5

FIGURE 1-2. Business Mindset Self-Assessment Test (continued)					
	Strongly Disagree	Often Disagree	Sometimes Agree	Often Agree	Strongly Agree
15. I am prepared to invest the necessary resources (time, effort, money) to build my business.	1	2	3	4	5
16. I don't put off until tomorrow what I need to do today.	1	2	3	4	5
17. I seek and accept constructive feedback.	1	2	3	4	5
18. I am respected by people in my industry, market, and community.	1	2	3	4	5
19. I have a well-thought-out and communicated business vision.	1	2	3	4	5
20. My company conducts weekly training sessions with employees.	1	2	3	4	5
21. I adjust, improve, or replace areas or activities whenever established performance levels are not met.	1	2	3	4	5
22. I know where to locate information on my target market and do so regularly.	1	2	3	4	5
23. I have written personal and business goals.	1	2	3	4	5
24. I value my business coaches and/or mentors.	1	2	3	4	5
25. I do what needs to be done today but maintain a long-term perspective on my business and personal life.	1	2	3	4	5
26. I promise only what I can, and will, deliver.	1	2	3	4	5
27. No person is an island, including me. I know I cannot run my business alone.	1	2	3	4	5
28. I understand the importance of sticking to a plan but remaining flexible.	1	2	3	4	5
29. My work ethic is consistent with my business goals.	1	2	3	4	5
30. I always try to find the good in situations and people.	1	2	3	4	5
TOTAL					

2. PLAN AND DEFINE YOUR BUSINESS

Now that you're becoming clearer about what it takes internally to operate a booming e-commerce business, it's time to articulate your vision and then begin moving down a logical action path to attain it. Yes, I know this is easier said than done. If you've read the introduction to this book, you know that I've already been there.

But now it's your turn. Grab a loose-leaf notebook or piece of paper and use it to paint a vivid picture of your ideal lifestyle; that is, identify the one or two things that you really want the most in this life and how your online business can help you get them.

For instance, do you wish to:

■ have more time with your family and friends?

■ move to a warmer climate?

■ enjoy more fulfilling relationships?

■ have a career that makes the most of your passions and strengths?

Now do the same thing, only this time focus on your e-commerce business. Ask yourself questions, such as:

■ What kind of an online business do I really want to create?

■ What types of products or services do I really want to sell? Are these different than what I'm currently offering (if applicable)?

■ What kind of business would make me excited to get up in the morning and go to work?

■ What am I most passionate about, and how can I turn that into an online business?

Once you've communicated your online business vision, go on an adventure! Check out what other people—those who share your dream—are doing and learn more about solid business practices.

3. CONDUCT SOME ONLINE RESEARCH

Go to your favorite search engine and look for your current product or service (or what you'd like to sell online). It's a good idea to pick one search engine (e.g., Google.com, Yahoo.com, AOL.com, Dogpile.com, MSN.com), and stick with it. Then, type in keywords and key phrases that your prospects might use to find you on the internet. For example, if your product is an e-book that instructs people on how to improve their golf swing you might try: "golf instruction," "golf lesson," "free golf lesson online," or "Tiger Woods." You get the idea. (By the way, I go into great detail on keywords and key phrases in Chapter 9.)

> ## Success is nothing more...
> than a few simple disciplines, practiced every day."
> —*Jim Rohn, author, motivational speaker, and business philosopher*

Once you've found several web sites, make note of what you liked or disliked about each: prices, tone and feel, products and services offered, and so on. Use your own notebook or the template I've provided (see Figure 1.3). You can also download the template from www.OnlineMarketingTemplates.com.

4. LEARN MORE ABOUT YOUR FELLOW ENTREPRENEURS

Go to my web site (www.MasteringOnlineMarketing.com) and listen to my interview with business expert Michael Gerber. He provides wonderful insights into the challenges that entrepreneurs face and how to overcome some of the most common pitfalls.

5. FIND AN ACCOUNTABILITY PARTNER

This is one of the best, and simplest, tools you'll ever find for staying focused and on track—and it's a part of every class I teach. Ask someone—a friend, family member, or colleague—to become your "accountability partner." It's even better if your partner is an online marketer as well; that way, you'll each have a sounding board for new ideas. Set up a regular time each week—a half

FIGURE 1-3. Research Template				
Name, Web Address, and Contact Information	Products and/or Services Offered and Pricing	Strengths	Weaknesses	How Did I Find This Site?

hour is usually sufficient—to meet in person or over the phone. Use the time to talk about what you've learned in the book and what actions you've taken as a result, or anything else you'd like to share—thoughts, questions, road-blocks, successes, and frustrations. Before you end each discussion, tell your partner what you'll accomplish before you meet again (e.g., read a certain number of chapters, improve something specific on your site, do some research, etc.). Begin each session with an update on your progress: Did you accomplish what you promised? If not, why not? Can you identify things that may be standing in your own way? If so, how can you overcome these?

CHAPTER 1 REMINDERS

Before moving on to Chapter 2, "Strategic Marketing: The Key to Sustainable Online Success," let's take a minute to review the most important lessons learned from this chapter:

- **Look before you leap.** Make sure that you've done your research before jumping in; you'll be glad you did.

- **Pay attention to detail, plan for the future, and be prepared to learn something new each day.** Business success is achieved through a minute-by-minute, hour-by-hour, day-by-day, week-by-week, month-by-month commitment to small, seemingly mundane tasks.

- **Seek support, advice, and help from others.** No man or woman is an island.

Visit my web site (www. Mastering OnlineMarketing.com) if you'd like to learn more. You'll find free up-to-the-minute blogs, advice, articles, templates, and resources.

> ## "Happiness is not in the mere possession
>
> of money; it lies in the joy of achievement, in the thrill of creative effort."
>
> —*Franklin D. Roosevelt, 32nd U.S. President*

CHAPTER 2

STRATEGIC MARKETING

The Key to Sustainable Online Success

In this chapter you'll learn

- *ways to gain control over your online business using superior marketing skills*

- *why it's vital that you view marketing as a process, not a project*

- *the two most important customer metrics*

- *why you should invest more time, energy, and imagination in the marketing process than money*

- *how to grow your online business geometrically*

- *why it's all about them, not you*

...and much more.

" **The best career advice to give to the young is...**

'Find out what you like doing best and get someone to pay you for doing it.'"

—*Katherine Whitehorn, British journalist*

As discussed in the last chapter, there's never been a better time to start an online business. The internet is booming and will continue to grow by leaps and bounds in the foreseeable future. If you offer your target audience a valuable product or service, treat your customers well, and develop your site skillfully, you'll greatly increase the odds of growing and maintaining a successful e-commerce business. But that's just the beginning; if profitable internet sales are your goal, you'll need to create ways to stand out from the crowd.

Consider this: Americans who live in or near metropolitan areas are exposed to an average of 3,500 marketing messages a day! This means that they are bombarded with 24,500 every week and 1.3 million each year. And because they're not willing, or able, to focus on each one of these, they listen up only when the communication is relevant and meaningful, and grabs their attention.

Common sense, you say? Absolutely. Understanding this is the easy part; figuring out *how* to do it is much tougher. It is even more difficult on the internet because in this age of information every Tom, Dick, and Harry is selling advice, products, or services. So while the world wide web provides a global sales channel, it also means you'll be competing head to head with national and international companies.

THE ROUGH-AND-TUMBLE ONLINE MARKETPLACE

Let's face it, today's online environment is tough and your site may be just one of thousands competing for the same prospects and customers. Entrepreneurs will run some of these businesses, while others will be operated by large corporations. Some will be effective; others will not—and many will have more money and far more experience than you.

Are you starting to think, "Why bother?" I hope not. Although it's important to be realistic about internet competition, your ability to compete on a level playing field with anyone—big or small—has never been better. No other sales vehicle in history has ever afforded a better opportunity for virtually anyone to start a truly competitive business inexpensively and quickly. And even though some of your online competitors will outspend you, they won't outdo you in areas where money doesn't count, if you learn and apply superior strategies and tactics. If you're willing to invest your time, energy, and imagination—instead of lots of money—to do so, you'll have no problem competing with the big guys!

The process for getting there begins in your head with a belief that excellent marketing provides the single greatest leverage (control) that you have for growing and sustaining a thriving online business.

WHAT IS MARKETING?

Marketing is everything you do to promote your company. It begins the moment you visualize your business and continues up to, and long after, your customers buy your products and/or services regularly. When done correctly, marketing is always intentional and detail oriented, and overlaps into every single part of your business, such as product or service selection, business location and environment, sales training, customer service policies, and how you answer the phone. It is not just a sale, or an order, or a customer, or a transaction. Instead, it is a multifaceted and continual process that develops over time.

I often discuss an invaluable tenet with my students and clients that was taught to me by one of my mentors, Jay Conrad Levinson, the father of Guerrilla Marketing. It is that they should view marketing as a continuous circle—one that begins with an idea for generating revenues and continues until a company has earned the repeated patronage of loyal and profitable customers. (You can listen to an audio clip of Jay Levinson at www.Mastering OnlineMarketing.com.) I also remind them that many entrepreneurs mistakenly view marketing differently. They view it as a straight line—one that begins with luring prospects to buy and ends with the sale.

In order to illustrate this concept, I've developed a list of nine marketing must-dos. In my opinion, adherence to them can literally make any business—online or otherwise. As you'll see, some are conceptual, others are more strategic in nature, and the rest are quite tactical (actionable), but they are all equally important.

THE NINE MOST CRITICAL MARKETING ATTITUDES AND ACTION STEPS

STEP 1: VIEW MARKETING AS A PROCESS, NOT A PROJECT

Smart online marketers understand that they must build and maintain long-term relationships with their high-value customers. This begins with offering superior products and services and ends with repeat purchases from devoted customers.

Achieving this lofty goal, however, takes much more than industry or product knowledge. In order to be profitable, you must be able to manage the two primary activities of any business: projects and processes. So what's the difference between the two?

Projects are unique, temporary, and have a beginning, middle, and end. For instance, developing your web site is a project. You start with an idea, get designs, build it, place it on a server, and launch it on the internet. Once the site is up, the project is over.

Conversely, *processes* are your business's ongoing activities. So while you've completed a project by getting your site up and running, you now need to develop a process for updating and maintaining it for as long as your online business exists. This also applies to marketing in a more general way. Building a marketing strategy may be a project, but implementing that strategy is a process. While each contains actionable tasks, projects are finite and processes can be duplicated and used over and over again.

How is this relevant to developing your online business? Simple. If you acknowledge the difference and manage the two successfully, it will make many of the challenges you face seem less daunting.

As I've said before, marketing is about building lasting relationships with loyal customers. It involves a commitment to serve, before, during, and after a sale. It's a process, not a project—one that requires a long-term perspective. It's not one transaction. It's not one order. It's not one anything. Rather, it's accepting the benefits of ongoing connections and doing whatever it takes to grow and nourish them. Like a good marriage, it begins with a sincere desire to please two people—you and your spouse—and continues with a constant commitment to make that happen. So while the wedding itself is a project, the marriage is a continual process—which must be fed and watered every day. If not, it usually fails.

In a more specific way, your marketing communications are a process. Consider this: Most experts agree that it takes between 9 and 27 marketing messages before a consumer moves from a prospect to a customer. Although estimates vary widely, one thing is sure: it takes more than one.

Can you make a sale with one ad? Sure. But the sale generally won't cover the ad's development cost. So what do most entrepreneurs do in this instance? They bail out before they should. After, you'll hear them say things like, "I wrote an article and posted it online and got nothing. It didn't work," or "I tried a pay-per-click campaign and almost lost my shirt. Don't try it." What's going on here? They're erroneously blaming the project concept for their failure to follow a winning process! How can I be so sure? Easy! There are thousands of online marketers who submit articles and use pay-per-click campaigns that effectively drive prospects (who convert to profitable customers) to their web site. The results are irrefutable. However, the processes used to complete the project may not be. For example, the article may have been poorly written and/or the pay-per-click campaign might not have been the best sales tool for the product. There are hundreds of potential reasons for failure. However, the most glaring mistake was that these entrepreneurs mistook a process for a project and stopped abruptly when they didn't get the results they expected.

If you're going to be successful, you have to be in it for the long term, not one-shot deals.

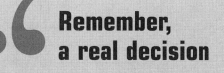

Remember, a real decision is measured by the fact that you've taken new action. If there's no action, you haven't truly decided."

—*Anthony Robbins, American life coach, writer, and professional speaker*

STEP 2: LEARN HOW TO GROW YOUR BUSINESS GEOMETRICALLY

One of the biggest mistakes that entrepreneurs make is focusing their entire marketing efforts on acquiring new customers. Not only does this strategy cost them far more than retaining current customers (estimates vary but most experts agree that it is four to nine times more expensive), but it take a great deal more effort because they constantly have to replace them. Recent commerce studies indicate that the average American company loses between 10 and 13 percent of its customer base each year. Therefore, in order to grow profitably, you must be prepared to concentrate on getting more from the customers you already have.

> ## Consumers will go where...
>
> they choose, and are invited, and stay where they're well treated."
>
> —*Mary Eule Scarborough, author, speaker, and marketing expert*

How? First, you need to understand that there are only four ways to grow any business. They are:

1. **Get new customers.** This is the only focus for many small businesses, which is ultimately a big mistake.

2. **Increase the average dollar amount per transaction.** For example, if your current average sale per customer is $10, then offering a logical $2 add-on ("Would you like some jewelry cleaner for your ring?") could increase your sales revenues substantially.

3. **Increase the average number of transactions per customer over a certain period of time**. Let's assume that you're an accountant whose typical customers come in once a year to have their taxes done. Then imagine how your revenues would grow if you convinced even some of your clients to use your service twice a year! You might offer to look over their finances every six months to let them know specific ways they could reduce their tax liability before the end of the year… you get the idea.

Also, don't hesitate to tell your customers how to use your products correctly. For example, many years ago sales of Prell shampoo grew substantially with the use of one word: *repeat*. Instead of instructing its customers to simply wash and rinse, the company added this one word. The rest is history.

4. **Increase the length of time your average customer stays loyal to your business.** If your standard client continues to buy from you for six months and you increase that to seven, eight, or even nine months, you will be delighted at your newfound revenue.

STEP 3: FIND AND USE THE TWO MOST IMPORTANT CUSTOMER METRICS

There is absolutely no way to develop and grow a successful online business—or any other one for that matter—if you can't accurately forecast your revenues and expenses. In order to do that, find out the answers to the following two questions:

1. What is one customer worth to me over his or her lifetime as my customer?

This, as they say, is where the rubber meets the road. Before you do anything else, you must find out what an average customer is worth to your business (their customer lifetime value, or CLV) and allow the answer to guide every marketing decision you make. It will tell you how much you can realistically spend to acquire a new customer (or keep a current one) and/or if your marketing plans and forecasts are realistic.

Calculate:

Take your average transaction amount (in dollars), multiply it by the average number of transactions per month/year, and multiply that by the number of months/years your average customer remains loyal to your business.

For example, let's assume that I have an online site where I sell a series of marketing e-books for $12 each. If a typical customer buys two of my books every year for three years, then I would simply multiply the three numbers together ($12 x 2/year x 3 years). In this instance my average CLV is $72.

2. What does it cost me to acquire a customer?

This will also remind you of how much it costs when you lose one.

Calculate:

Add up all of the direct marketing and advertising dollars you've spent and divide it by the number of new customers you acquired as a result. So, using the previous example, let's say I sent 1,500 direct mail pieces to qualified prospects, inviting them to log on to my web site and purchase an e-book. Let's also assume that it cost me a total of $1,000: $100 for paper; $150 for creative services (design and copywriting); $300 for printing; and $450 for postage. If I got 15 people to purchase an e-book as a result of this effort, it means that each new customer cost me $67 (and resulted in a mere $180 in revenue).

The result? A losing proposition. I spent $1,000 and made $180. However, since I know that each of my new 15 customers will spend a total of $72 with me over his or her lifetime, I can reasonably expect to receive gross revenues of $1,080 over the next three years. While this is better than losing money, it's still not good enough.

Using What You Have Learned

The goal then is to balance these two numbers. Look for ways to increase your CLV and decrease the costs associated with obtaining new customers (and you're in luck, because there are lots of low-cost, effective ways to market over the internet).

If your online business is new and you don't have access to this information, make an educated guess. Use conservative industry and consumer behavior data to guide you. Once you find the answers, write (or type) them on a piece of paper and make several extra copies. Pin one on your shirt, tape one to your forehead, attach one to your computer, make one into a refrigerator magnet, and have another printed on your favorite coffee mug.

STEP 4: DEVELOP A SOLID STRATEGIC AND TACTICAL PLAN

As I discussed in the last chapter, most entrepreneurs are action oriented. Rather than sitting around thinking and hoping, they get out there and make things happen, which is a good thing. However, problems occur when they do the wrong things the right way or do the right things the wrong way. The object, of course, is to *do the right things the right way*. And since we've already established that marketing is a process, not a transaction, you'll need to begin by developing a *written marketing plan.*

A marketing plan is a blue print, a road map, and a tool for keeping you and your business on track. Vitally important to the health of any business, it is often developed as part of a full-blown business plan and should be reviewed and updated often. Before beginning, you should know the answers to the following four questions:

1. *What are the products and/or services I'll offer?*

2. *What are the main features and benefits of my product or service?*

3. *Who are my targeted prospects?* What problem do they have and how will I solve it? Is the universe of qualified prospects—people who want or need my product and have the ability and desire to purchase it—large enough to sustain sales and profits over the long term?

4. *Who is my competition?* What do they do better, or worse, than me?

When you're ready to write your marketing plan, I strongly suggest that you check out David and Mary Scarborough's book, *The Procrastinator's Guide to Marketing: A Pain-Free Solution that Delivers a Profit-Producing Marketing Plan* (Irvine, CA: Entrepreneur, 2007). Mary and her husband David have created a simple yet comprehensive marketing plan formula and outline. They masterfully remove the intimidation factor and make it easy for anyone to develop this vital business document. You can also visit their web site if you'd like to download their outline; go to www. StrategicMarketingAdvisors.com.

There are two main sections in a marketing plan—one with a *strategic* focus and another that's more *tactical*. Very briefly, the strategic portion of your plan will include the following:

■ information about you and/or your company—who you are and why you're in business

■ the products or services you'll offer for sale

■ your long- and short-term prioritized goals and objectives

- an assessment of your current situation and identification of internal and external factors that may impact your ability to achieve your objectives (positively or negatively)
- what you'll do to achieve your goals
- the costs associated with your plan and the method you'll use for measuring success.

The tactical part of your plan provides details on your marketing activities—exactly what you'll do and when. For example, in this section you'll answer the following types of questions:

1. What are the specific sales channels I'll use to achieve my goals? (e.g., pay-per-clicks, online banner ads, newspaper ads that drive people to my web site, affiliate programs, etc.)?

2. What are the communication methods I'll use to ensure that my targeted audience hears about me, gains confidence in my ability to solve its most pressing problems, and is compelled to accept my invitation to act?

Because every online business is unique in some ways, your tactics will vary. In all cases, however, they must support the goals that you identified in the first section. Unfortunately, many entrepreneurs focus on these tactics before they develop their strategy, making them more likely to do the right things the wrong way or the wrong things the right way.

Important: Don't Skip Strategic Planning!

After many years of consulting with clients, I've learned that advising entrepreneurs to create a written plan is the very last thing they want to hear. After they utter their first loud groan, they usually turn on their heels and take off running in the opposite direction—fast. Why? Because writing can be intimidating; planning can be tedious and boring; and many people believe that it's unnecessary anyway. They erroneously believe that it's a waste of time to stop doing in order to sit down and think about what to do and how to do it… after all, nothing's getting done, right?

Wrong. Estimates range, but many experts believe that the mere act of writing down a goal increases the odds of achieving it by 15 to 30 percent.

Quick Tips for Writing Your Own Marketing Plan

DO:

- **Write it.** The mere act of putting it on paper increases your chances of succeeding substantially.
- **Update it regularly.** As they say, stuff happens. Stay flexible and change your plan as circumstances warrant.
- **Put a time line on it.** Your plan must be for a specified period of time, preferably at least one year.
- **Track how well you're doing.** Compare your actual results against your original forecasts. How did you do? Were your predictions too aggressive, on target, or not challenging enough?
- **Make sure your goals are realistic and attainable.** Do you have the time, money, and resources to achieve your objectives?

DON'T:

- **Worry about making it long or fancy.** You won't get extra points for length or formality.
- **Think it's a waste of time.** A marketing plan is your business's best friend. Don't underestimate its value!

STEP 5: KNOW YOUR TARGET MARKET AND FIND YOUR NICHE

The internet is jam-packed with competition. Therefore, as with most things, it's far easier, less costly, and more effective to be a big fish in a small pond rather than a big fish in a big pond. Think of it this way: Trying to get everyone's attention is similar to trying to get someone to notice you splashing in the middle of the ocean. You'd have far more luck getting some people—those who are ready to buy what you're selling—to notice the big splash you've made in a small puddle.

Additionally, it's important to note that people who shop online are looking for a specific product or service that solves their individual problem. Your job is to accurately identify that need; provide a real solution; get their attention and make it easy for them to say yes. The best way to do this is to create a niche for your business and *own it.*

Here are some examples:

■ a physician who specializes in geriatric medicine

■ a lawyer who specializes in collaborative divorces

■ an artist who specializes in medical drawings

■ an e-book writer who specializes in books about parrots

■ an employment advisor who specializes in interviewing skills

■ a child psychologist who specializes in potty-training techniques

In order to find a niche, begin by asking yourself, "Who wants or needs what I have to offer?" (Clue: The wrong answer is "Everyone.") The next thing to do is narrow down the universe of prospects. How old are they? Does your product or service appeal more to men, women, or children? What makes this group unique?

Once you've answered those questions, you'll need to go even further, because e-commerce businesses operate in a very different environment than brick-and-mortar companies. While more traditional business owners have to search for prospects, online marketers have consumers searching for them!

> ## " The difference between great people and everyone else...
>
> is that great people create their lives actively, while everyone else is created by their lives, passively waiting to see where life takes them next. The difference between the two is the difference between living fully and just existing."
>
> —*Michael Gerber, author of* The E-Myth

Therefore it's a good idea to pick a product or service that people want *and* are prepared to buy right now.

Conversely, if you haven't selected a product or service to offer yet, start with something that interests you, do some market research, and work backward. For example, let's say you've done some research and confirmed that there are a growing number of city apartment dwellers who have, or are looking to buy, a poogle (a beagle-poodle hybrid). In this case, you should ask yourself what product or service might benefit this group of people. A dog-walking service? An e-book titled *The Care and Feeding of Poogles*? Gourmet poogle treats? Designer poogle sweaters? Poogle beds? The list is endless.

STEP 6: FOCUS ON CONVEYING BENEFITS, NOT FEATURES

People do not like to be sold; yet they love to buy. Although it's wise to provide your prospects with relevant information about your products and services, they want to be encouraged to make their own decisions, not have them jammed down their throats! Therefore, if you understand consumer psychology—that is, why people buy—then you'll be better able to articulate your product's or service's most important benefits. So if you think you're going to get smart consumers to purchase what you're selling by using glitzy words, flashy effects, over-the-top claims, screechy headlines, and amateurish copy, think again. These tactics don't work and actually undermine your credibility with your prospects and customers.

Instead, your marketing should aim at building and maintaining trust and confidence in you, your company, and the products and services you offer. This must happen before you invite a purchase and begins with understanding and communicating their truths. Once you have uncovered them, you can develop your marketing campaign around addressing them and truly stand out from the rest.

So What Do Consumers Really Want?

People want to love and be loved. They want to enjoy good health. They want to be entertained. They want to be popular. They want to keep their children safe. They want to be challenged. They want to feel sexy. They want to look young. They want to be rich. They want their pain to stop. They want more freedom. They want to save time. They want to be respected.

As you've probably noticed, these desires are intangible; they can't be manufactured and packaged neatly inside a glass bottle. But they—and a host of others—lie at the heart of every purchase people make. They may buy a feature (a fast car, an ergonomic chair, a glossy lipstick, a real estate course), but

What Are People Buying?

Your customers do not buy because they're being marketed to or sold to. Instead, they buy because you help them realize the merits of owning what you offer.

- They buy promises you make. So make them with care.

- They buy your credibility or don't buy if you lack it.

- They buy solutions to their problems.

- They buy wealth, safety, success, security, love, and acceptance.

- They buy the consistency they've seen you exhibit.

- They buy value, which is not the same as price.

- They buy certainty. They buy your identity as conveyed by your marketing.

- They buy good taste and know it from bad taste.

- They buy the confidence you display in your own business.

—*Jay Conrad Levinson,* The Truth About Customers
(www.gmarketing.com)

what they're really buying is the benefit (sexy appearance, pain-free back, beauty, wealth). Therefore, effective marketers must learn to communicate benefits rather than just features—one of the most difficult things for many entrepreneurs to do. That's why it's so important to take as much time as you need to find out what your targeted prospects really want, not what you want to tell them. It's not necessary to compile a long list; quality matters, not quantity. Just make sure the benefits you identify are accurate and important to them, not you.

Trust me, consumers could care less about how long you've been in business, how many computers you have, or whether your company is family owned and operated. Additionally, overused phrases like "friendly service" and "quality products" are meaningless. Be specific!

Once you've uncovered your product's or service's key benefits, look them over and ask yourself if there's anything on the list that is a truly unique benefit—one that few (even better, none) of your competitors offers. If so, you've just completed the first step in developing your own unique selling proposition, or USP.

What Is a USP?

A unique selling proposition is a message that communicates, in clear and simple language, what sets you apart from your competitors. In other words, it answers this question: Why would someone be foolish to do business with my competitors over me?

what do they like abt. me.

Don't know? *Find out.* Not doing anything better than your competitors? *Come up with something, or face extinction.* Ask current customers what they like about doing business with you. Ask friends and colleagues to share with you their joys and frustrations regarding companies in your industry. Go online and check out the competition; ask yourself how you could go one better. Ask yourself if there's a need in your industry that isn't being filled and how you can act on it. After you come up with one, ask yourself one final question: How many of my competitors can say the same thing? If the answer is none, congratulations. If not, it's back to the drawing board.

You don't necessarily have to be the only one meeting a certain need, but you should be the only one articulating it! For instance, FedEx was not the only company that delivered overnight letters and packages, but it was the first to own that service (i.e., "When it absolutely, positively has to be there overnight"). There's no sense in inviting people to your web site if it's not set up as an effective marketing tool, so among other things, make sure you communicate your distinct benefits.

" For all the bells and whistles...

of internet marketing, technology marketing, and direct-response marketing, I really think it comes down to something really simple. *Whatever they're buying, you're selling.* In other words, your job is to not take a product and ram it down peoples' throats. Your job, and sometimes the challenge, is to find out what people want to buy, and not only allow them to buy it from you, but give them a unique, sustainable advantage for doing so.

In the marketplace today, with all the competition on the internet—more than ever, you have to have what's called a sustainable advantage.... You can't just have an edge over your competitors, because society now moves at internet speed. They're going to knock off that competitive advantage overnight unless it's what's called a sustainable competitive advantage. A sustainable uniqueness means that you're able to sustain it over a period of time because there's a barrier to entry. In other words, there's some reason that your competitors cannot easily match the unique value, the unique benefit, the unique proposition you're offering to your customers.

—Marlon Sanders, e-marketer and creator of "The Amazing Formula (www.PushButtonLetters.com.)

STEP 7: USE AN ASSORTMENT OF MARKETING TACTICS

Whether your goal is to produce profitable sales, achieve high-level aware-ness, or generate interest in your brick-and-mortar business, you need to choose your online, and offline, marketing tactics carefully. Since this book is devoted to helping you build and maintain a successful e-commerce busi-ness, I go into great detail in later chapters on ways you can get more traf-fic to your site and convert the visitors into paying customers. I demystify many online tools—search engine optimization and converting keywords and key phrases; pay-per-click ad campaigns; e-mail lists; the ins and outs of Google AdWords; directories; blogs and forums; and more—and encourage you to use a minimum of five devices to attract the right people to your online business.

> ## "We are the creative force of our life...
>
> and through our own decisions rather than our con-ditions, if we carefully learn to do certain things, we can accomplish those goals."
>
> —*Stephen Covey, author of*
> The Seven Habits of Highly Effective People

However, many people log on to an e-commerce site because of information they've received offline—that is, from more tradi-tional communication sources like newspaper ads, fliers, business cards, specialty products, and so on. So if you want to increase your chances of building a thriving online business, get offline people excited as well. In addition to including your web address boldly on every thing you do, from business cards to radio ads (and everything in between), there are many cre-ative, low-cost, high-impact methods for directing folks to your online busi-ness aside from the more traditional vehicles such as catalogs, newsletters, and classified ads.

For instance, maybe you've never considered the impact a well-placed feature article in your local newspaper might have on your e-commerce business. Remember, editors want stories as much as you want business, and they're usually willing to run a local-businessperson-makes-good story if it's interesting and not too self-serving. Or how about running a small ad in the classified section of your newspaper that offers a free taste of your product? You could invite folks to log on to your site and download a free report on the ten most important things to consider before selling your home or the 50 best homebased businesses to start. The key to this strategy, however, is that when readers get to your site, the information they find must be better than what they expect, not a thinly veiled sales pitch. There's no better way to obtain instant credibility than overdelivering—and in this case, it's done with content.

STEP 8: MAKE A GREAT FIRST IMPRESSION

I am constantly amazed at the number of people who seem oblivious to the effect their actions, demeanor, appearance, body language, and speech have on others, especially the first time around. This is even more baffling since research study after research study confirms that most people make judgments about someone's credibility, quality, and likeableness within seconds of meeting him or her for the first time. That's why there's no excuse for continuing to blow important meetings or miss golden opportunities, particularly given the plethora of available information devoted to helping people improve their ability to make great first impressions.

Although experts say tactics such as a firm handshake, warm smile, attentive gaze, and non-threatening body language make it easier to achieve, the secret to a good first impression is more intangible and revolves around *helping others feel good about themselves.* This occurs when we convey appreciation, express a positive attitude, communicate a mutual bond, or offer new and relevant information. It is the same for marketing all business, especially online ones: make a great first impression or risk extinction. Acknowledging this truth and knowing what to do about it are entirely different matters. But don't worry; you'll find lots of advice and tips to help you out in Chapters 4 and 5. For now, it's most important to acknowledge that first impressions are vitally important to the health of your online business, then do everything in your power to ensure that first-time visitors instantly like and trust you.

STEP 9: REMAIN FLEXIBLE AND ADAPT TO AN EVER-CHANGING MARKETPLACE

The online landscape is constantly changing. Nothing stays the same for long. What works well today may not work well tomorrow. Expect change. Prepare for change. Welcome change.

For example, just a couple of years ago, pop-up ads were the rage and actually quite effective… that is, until all the major browsers provided free blockers. Discouraging as this was for many online marketers, most adapted quickly and simply used other methods (e.g., better traffic and conversion strategies, meatier offers, pay-per-click campaigns, etc.) for increasing their sales. They embraced change and made it their ally, not their enemy.

> **Become a possibilitarian.**
>
> No matter how dark things seem to be or actually are, raise your sights and see possibilities—always see them, for they're always there."
>
> —*Dr. Norman Vincent Peale, orator and author*

WEB WORK: YOUR INTERACTIVE ADVENTURE

1. CALCULATE YOUR MARKETING IQ

Now that you have a better understanding about the vital role your skills, interests, and personality play in the success of your online business, it's time to identify your own marketing mindset strengths and weaknesses. To help you with this, I've developed a 30-item marketing self-assessment test. Like the business mindset assessment in the previous chapter, it is a useful way to gain revealing insights into your marketing strengths and weaknesses, in 15 minutes or less (see Figure 2-1).

Answer each question honestly, and you'll discover what beliefs and/or behaviors will help you build and maintain a profitable online business, as well as the ones that may be standing in your way. After you've finished the quiz, add up your score and refer to the "Score Interpretation" section that follows to see how well you've done. Although this assessment is very general

FIGURE 2-1. Marketing Mindset Self-Assessment Test

Name: _____   Date: _____

Company: _____

Directions: Circle the appropriate number for each statement listed. Once completed, add up your scores. Then refer to the interpretation section at the end to see where you stand. This is a wonderfully easy way to learn your strategic marketing mindset strengths and weaknesses.

Please note: In order to improve accuracy, the statements are not grouped and do not appear in any particular order.

	Strongly Disagree	Often Disagree	Sometimes Agree	Often Agree	Strongly Agree
1. If I surveyed my customers today, they would agree that I follow up in a consistent and timely manner.	1	2	3	4	5
2. My communication, attitudes, and actions are all intentional and based on my marketing goals.	1	2	3	4	5
3. My friends, prospects, and customers would all say I am enthusiastic and consistently positive in all my interactions.	1	2	3	4	5
4. I build strong one-to-one relationships with my prospects and customers.	1	2	3	4	5
5. I consistently use my imagination to develop marketing strategies that are unconventional.	1	2	3	4	5
6. My business is oriented to giving. I make generosity a part of my overall marketing plan.	1	2	3	4	5
7. I actively work on developing marketing partnerships with other businesses.	1	2	3	4	5
8. I look for ways to amaze my customers with exceptional service.	1	2	3	4	5
9. I focus on having a clearly defined marketing niche.	1	2	3	4	5
10. I consistently use a marketing calendar to track and measure the effectiveness of my marketing weapons.	1	2	3	4	5
11. I have a clear and specific marketing plan that guides my weekly action steps.	1	2	3	4	5
12. I am fervently devoted to following up with my customers and prospects.	1	2	3	4	5

FIGURE 2-1. Marketing Mindset Self-Assessment Test (continued)

	Strongly Disagree	Often Disagree	Sometimes Agree	Often Agree	Strongly Agree
13. Instead of focusing on sales, I am dedicated to building long-term relationships.	1	2	3	4	5
14. Instead of thinking about what I can take from others, I built my business on a foundation of serving others.	1	2	3	4	5
15. It's important to deliver on your promises.	1	2	3	4	5
16. I spend time each week improving my marketing capabilities.	1	2	3	4	5
17. I can articulate my competitive advantages.	1	2	3	4	5
18. I know where to locate information on my target market.	1	2	3	4	5
19. My company has many different supplemental products in addition to its core offerings.	1	2	3	4	5
20. I keep information on my current customers and prospects.	1	2	3	4	5
21. I remain flexible and adjust to the changing environment.	1	2	3	4	5
22. I know what it costs me to retain a valuable customer.	1	2	3	4	5
23. I empower employees to do whatever it takes to please our customers.	1	2	3	4	5
24. I understand that some customers are more valuable than others.	1	2	3	4	5
25. I study other successful online businesses to learn ways to improve.	1	2	3	4	5
26. I understand the difference between my products' features and their benefits.	1	2	3	4	5
27. I keep track of current trends on the internet.	1	2	3	4	5
28. I look for ways to improve myself as a person.	1	2	3	4	5
29. I do whatever it takes to delight my customers.	1	2	3	4	5
30. I am an optimist and see possibilities in all situations.	1	2	3	4	5
TOTAL					

in nature, it will provide you with valuable knowledge that will help you as you build your e-commerce business, even if your score indicates that you would benefit from assistance from professionals such as a career coach, a business consultant, or a financial planner.

Score Interpretation

If your total points equal 75 or less, your marketing mindset needs improving. The good news, however, is that you have a wonderful opportunity to grow and learn, and it starts right here.

If your score is between 76 and 119, you've got an average marketing mindset. You could realistically expect to improve your overall online business performance by carefully following the strategies and tactics presented in this book.

If your total points equal 120 or more, good for you! You've got the right marketing attitude goals. But now is not the time to rest; take advantage of the strategies and tactics presented in this guide to make your online business soar.

2. USE LOW-COST OR FREE GUERRILLA MARKETING WEAPONS

If you're a student of Guerrilla marketing, you're already aware that there are hundreds of marketing weapons you can use to merge your online and offline strategies. I've listed 20 of my favorites below, but there are many more. (To obtain a free list of the 100 most effective marketing weapons visit my web site at www.gmarketingcoach.com.) How many of these are you using?

1. Free samples, consultations, seminars
2. Articles and columns with meaty, informative tips and advice
3. One or more robust referral programs
4. Weekly sales and customer service training
5. A customer care handbook for every employee
6. A truly unique selling proposition that is communicated often
7. Personal non-selling customer communication (e.g., phone calls, letters)

8. A simple direct marketing web site

9. An informative marketing on-hold phone message

10. A real live person who greets your callers promptly, professionally, and cheerfully

11. After-hours availability via fax, e-mail, web site, emergency on-call staff

12. Weekly or monthly newsletters

13. Participation in local business groups

14. Joint ventures or strategic partnerships

15. Downloadable pdf file with useful content

16. Content-rich audio on your web site

17. Personalized e-mail signature

18. Proactive customer "oops" letter and gift for when things don't go right

19. Participation in community events

20. Proactive thank-you letter and gift for high-value customers

3. OBTAIN CANDID FEEDBACK

If you already have an online or offline business, invite at least three people to experience your company's customer service, product selection, return policies, web site, location, and so on, and provide honest feedback and suggestions for improvement. (Better yet, have them choose three other people—ones you don't know—to do the same. And make sure they don't tell you who they are or when they'll do this.)

4. TURN YOUR PRODUCT AND/OR SERVICE FEATURES INTO BENEFITS

Following is a simple example and blank template that will help you turn your product and/or service features into benefits, using the transitional phrase *which means that.* You'll want to include these benefits in all of your marketing communications. Here's how it might look for a new car:

FEATURE	TRANSITION	BENEFIT
Driver side and passenger airbags	*which means that…*	You and your family will feel safe and secure.
Ergonomic seat	*which means that…*	Your back won't be sore.
Gets 40 miles per gallon	*which means that…*	You won't go broke paying for gas.
Sleek styling	*which means that…*	You'll look sexy driving your new car.

Now it's your turn.

FEATURE	TRANSITION	BENEFIT
	which means that…	
	which means that…	
	which means that…	
	which means that…	
	which means that…	
	which means that…	
	which means that…	

CHAPTER 2 REMINDERS

Before moving on to Chapter 3, "Products and Services: The Key to Smart Selling," let's take a minute to review the most important lessons learned from this chapter:

- Projects are unique and temporary; processes are ongoing activities.
- The two most important metrics to know are your average CLV (customer lifetime value) and how much it costs you to obtain one customer.
- Don't try to be all things to all people; carve out a niche for your online business and do your best to own it.
- Visit my web site, www.Mastering OnlineMarketing.com, if you'd like to learn more about developing a winning marketing mindset. You'll find free up-to-the-minute blogs, advice, articles, templates, and resources.

> **" I'm a great believer in luck.**
>
> And the harder I work, the more I have of it."
>
> —*Stephan Leacock, writer and humorist*

PRODUCTS AND SERVICES

The Key to Smart Selling

In this chapter you'll learn

- *how to avoid committing the three biggest online product mistakes*

- *ways to ensure that people are actively seeking what you're selling*

- *how to design your offer using a marketing funnel approach*

- *ways to leverage your products and services to save time and create multiple streams of income*

...and much more.

> ## "A lot of companies have chosen to downsize...
>
> and maybe that was the right thing for them. We chose a different path. Our belief was that if we kept putting great products in front of customers, they would continue to open their wallets."
>
> —*Steve Jobs, CEO of Apple Computer*

In this chapter I provide you with a simple step-by-step process for assessing the marketplace and choosing a winning product or service offering—a vital strategy for achieving online success. I have personally coached and/or consulted with hundreds of entrepreneurs who started out with big dreams of selling superb products and/or services over the internet. Over time, however, their dreams turned into nightmares as these very smart people joined the ever-growing group of online fatalities. And, in addition to the ones I've covered in previous chapters, one of their biggest mistakes was that they bought into the prevalent get-rich-quick internet hype, which led them to believe that they could pick something—*anything*—to sell and they'd make a fortune. This couldn't be further from the truth.

> ## A market is never saturated...
>
> with a good product, but it is very quickly saturated with a bad one."
>
> —*Henry Ford, American industrialist*

Today's internet is jam-packed with competition that's growing at an alarming rate. That's why you'll have to be much smarter if you're going to succeed. And when it comes to selecting a product or service offering, you'll need to do your homework instead of chasing opportunity. So first, let's start with a simple illustration.

AVOIDING THE GOLD RUSH MENTALITY

In 1840, few Americans had ever seen that faraway land known as California. However, by 1845, wagons and ships were bringing more and more easterners into the new frontier. A wealthy Swiss immigrant, John Sutter, arrived in California in 1839 and was quickly absorbed with building a massive agricultural business on his new land. He was therefore pleased to see newcomers—after all, they provided cheap labor for his growing business.

However, on January 24, 1848, Sutter's plan started to unravel when one of his employees, James Marshall, was completing construction of a sawmill about 50 miles northeast of his ranch near the American River, and noticed something shiny. It turned out to be a pea-sized piece of gold. And the rest, as they say, is history.

Although Marshall and his men continued to find more gold, he and Sutter were more interested in finishing the sawmill and knew that gold diggers would impede their progress. So they decided to stay quiet about their discovery. Then in walked Sam Brennan, a talented opportunist, who grew rich by exploiting the inevitable onslaught of gold-hungry miners. After purchasing all of the picks, pans, and shovels available, he dashed through San Francisco's streets and boldly announced the great discovery, waving a bottle of gold dust as proof.

As word spread, Californians flocked to the river armed with their dreams and mining equipment. And whom did they buy it from? You guessed it: Sam Brennan, who knew exactly how to apply basic supply-and-demand principles and sold mining equipment to crazed prospectors at exorbitant markups. In less than ten weeks, he became a wealthy man. A new era was born.

In 1849, thousands of Americans (as well as Europeans and South Americans) headed west, seeking a lifetime of wealth in exchange for a year of hard work. And while there were a few lucky souls—just enough to keep the dream alive—most gave up and went home after months, or years, of backbreaking labor. In addition to dwindling supplies, the gold was embedded deep into hard rock, making panning less and less effective. And so it is with the internet. Like the riverbeds it is a *free market*—accessible to anyone as long as they have time, tools, and work ethic.

Yes, there are several online businesses that have made it "overnight" (e.g., Google, Yahoo, MySpace, YouTube, hosting ISPs, etc.), but they're the rare exception. The rest of us have to be smarter. We must do our research, keep our fingers on the pulse of our targeted prospects, and anticipate their future needs. It isn't that easy anymore. So today, thousands, even millions, are flocking to the internet looking to get rich overnight. The marketplace is saturated, and profitable customers—the gold—are getting harder to find.

Although this paradigm shift took place over several decades, major changes in the internet can occur in months or less. So, like the miners of the 1800s, you'll need to dig deeper and search for a problem that you can fix with your outstanding product or service—and, as I said in Chapter 2, the more specific the niche, the better (e.g., offering products and/or services for a particular breed instead of just dogs).

So remember, although there are plenty of get-rich-quick schemes on the internet, they are very similar to America's gold rush lore. Don't fall for them. Rather, find a problem or need, then sell the "picks and shovels" necessary to alleviate it.

THREE BIG MISTAKES ONLINE MARKETERS COMMIT

I offer you the following three big mistakes that many online marketers make when choosing what products or services to offer. Avoid them at all costs.

1. CHASING OPPORTUNITY INSTEAD OF PASSION

You need passion—fervor and excitement—to carry you through the tough times. Identify and articulate your interests first, then see if you can build a business around them. For example, if you're passionate about saving the environment, write an e-book on green cleaning products or ways to recycle trash.

2. DEVELOPING A PRODUCT BEFORE FINDING AN AUDIENCE

Although you have a product, you may not have an audience. Although you have an interest, you may be the only one. If you build an online business around a product or service that no one wants, needs, or is actively seeking, you're in big trouble. So while you should begin with your passion, make sure others share it.

3. EXPECTING AND ASKING FOR A SALE ON THE FIRST VISIT

Remember, marketing is a relationship-building process, not a transaction. It can take months, even years, to develop and is a lot like dating. Imagine this: You've just met a very nice person who has asked you out on a first date. Since you like him or her and are quite interested, you gladly say yes, and off you go to dinner at a lovely restaurant.

As you enter the dining room, you look into your date's eyes and are immediately glad you've accepted the invitation. However, just after you sit down at your table, your date says, "Will you marry me?" If you're like most people, you scream "WHHAATT?" then get up from the table and run as fast as you can in the opposite direction!

Sound silly? In this context, perhaps, but it's the same reaction many online consumers have when they're asked to buy on their very first web site visit!

Why doesn't this work? Because internet marketing is a lot like building a personal relationship—it takes *time, effort, and commitment* to build *trust, rapport, and a lasting friendship.*

And while there are exceptions to this rule (e.g., your prospects are pre-sold, you sell a product that people buy on impulse, and/or you offer products that people need right now), you should be prepared to take your prospects on a first,

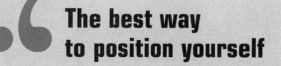

**The best way
to position yourself**

as a leader in your industry is to have your own signature product. And with today's technology it is easier than you would ever imagine."

—*Mitch Meyerson and Michael Port,
co-founders, The 90 Day Product Factory
(www.90DayProduct.com)*

second, third, and maybe even sixth "date" before you invite them to purchase.

So read on. I'm going to show you a system that will help you make the sale—and many more to come!

HOW TO CHOOSE A PRODUCT OR SERVICE TO SELL

Now that you're better prepared to begin the selection process, it's time to act. Using the following four steps will make it much easier.

STEP 1: TURN YOUR INTEREST INTO A PRODUCT OR SERVICE

Although the words product and service are often used interchangeably, they are two different types of offerings. **Products** are normally considered concrete or **tangible**—they can be touched or seen. Examples include cars, books, e-zines, computers, and so on. **Services** are intangible and can be valued only after they are delivered.

Examples of common online services include:

- **Consultation and/or Coaching.** Professional advice and guidance delivered online or over the telephone
- **Tele-classes.** Live, interactive workshops conducted over the telephone (similar to conference calls)
- **Subscriptions.** Paid enrollment for access to a wide array of information

Criteria for Choosing

First, consider the best fit given your lifestyle, talents, interests, and desire for passive or active income. For example, if you don't like to write and/or can't hire someone who does, you'll probably want to steer clear of creating e-books.

Next, examine the start-up costs associated with bringing your product or service to the online marketplace. For example, will you have to maintain a certain level of product inventory? Or, does your particular service offering require certification training?

Finally, go online and check out the types of current products and services available for your interest area.

Keep in mind that you can develop one, two, or a combination of products and services! However, in the beginning I suggest focusing on one or two until you've gained more experience. Once you have an idea of what you'd like to do, it's time for Step 2.

STEP 2: MAKE SURE PEOPLE ARE ACTIVELY SEARCHING FOR YOUR PRODUCT OR SERVICE IDEA

Now that you've selected your offering type, it's time to make sure you don't spend months and months developing a product or service, only to learn that no one wants to buy it! So, before going any further, you want to make sure that

- enough people are actively looking for it
- you can achieve profitable sales
- the marketplace isn't oversaturated with competition
- you develop a product niche that you can own.

Although there are numerous ways to obtain this information—too many to cover in this chapter—following are two very easy ways to get answers quickly.

Find out how many people are looking for your product or service

Use the "keyword selector tool" located at http://inventory.overture.com. Type in words or phrases related to your product or service—ones that you think your target audience would use to find it (e.g. "Panasonic 50" plasma TV," "midlife crisis," "Kansas barbeque sauce"). You'll receive a list of the approximate number of times your word or phrase was searched for during a recent month. You can also double-click on any word or phrase to drill down even further.

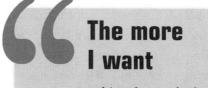

The more I want

to get something done... the less I call it work."

—*Richard Bach, American writer*

Your results will understandably depend on the size of your pond. Broader terms, such as "marketing" (around 224,000 when I checked), "coins" (around 214,000), and "golf" (around 625,000) will have larger numbers. Sounds great, doesn't it? Not necessarily. Remember, your goal is to get **highly focused and targeted prospects** to your web site, not just warm bodies. For instance, you wouldn't want all 214,000 coin collectors visiting your site if you specialized only in Indian Head pennies. You get the idea.

Take a Look at the Competition

Next, learn as much as you can about your competitors. To do so, go to www.Google.com and type in the same keywords you used in the previous activity. Then visit the recommended web sites by clicking on the links provided in the results list. Check out the companies' products and/or service. How do they compare with yours? Are they priced similarly? Do they have a wider, or narrower, selection?

Then look for ways to make your site stand out by continuing to peel back the onion even further. Try to uncover products that appeal to the same target market (your audience size will be smaller, but you'll attract more qualified prospects) or meet unfulfilled needs. Alternatively, drill down even further and become the expert in a specific service area. For example, although your recycling consultation services might be beneficial to the entire planet, you might be better off specializing in recycling solutions in dry climates.

Case Study: The Quiche Story

A couple of years ago one of my Guerrilla Marketing coaches created a very lucrative online business using this two-step method. He was interested in providing cooking recipes for quiche. He went to http://inventory.overture.com and typed in the keyword "quiche" as shown in Figure 3-1.

Imagine his surprise when he received the results (see Figure 3-2) that indicated that there had been 9,294 searches for that keyword for one month only (September 2003). He was even more astonished when he discovered that there were 7,677 searches for the phrase "quiche recipe." This was his first aha! moment.

FIGURE 3-1.

Keyword Selector Tool

Not sure what search terms to bid on?
Enter a term related to your site and we will show you:

● Related searches that include your term

● How many times that term was searched on last month

Get suggestions for: (may take up to 30 seconds)

Quiche ▶

Note: All suggested search terms are subject to our standard editorial review process.

http://inventory.overture.com

FIGURE 3-2.

Get suggestions for: (may take up to 30 seconds)

Note: All suggested search terms are subject to our standard editorial review process.

Searches done in September 2003	
Count	**Search Term**
9294	quiche
7677	quiche recipe
1250	spinach quiche
1241	quiche lorraine
741	crustless quiche
646	quiche recipe spinach
369	lorraine quiche recipe
340	crustless quiche recipe
287	breakfast quiche
279	broccoli quiche
249	mini quiche recipe
233	zucchini quiche
218	quiche receipes
217	ham and cheese quiche
209	carb low quiche
199	crab quiche
198	quiche mini
185	seafood quiche
180	low fat quiche
170	quiche vegetable

http://inventory.overture.com/d/searchinventory/suggestion/

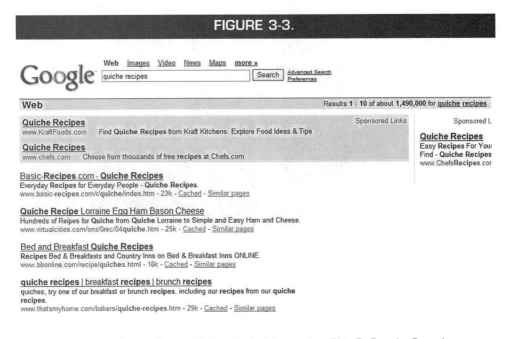

FIGURE 3-3.

www.google.com/search?hl=en&q=quiche+recipes&btnG=Google+Search

Now that he knew he had a viable niche, the next step was to find out how many quiche recipes and/or recipe books were available online. So he went to www.Google.com and typed in "quiche recipes." Once again, he was startled—and pleased—to find so few recipe sources available (see Figure 3-3). It was his second aha!

He knew he was on to something, so he began gathering quiche recipes from people over the internet. Over time he collected enough to create an affordable downloadable e-book, which earned him thousands of dollars in a relatively short period of time.

While I don't guarantee that you'll make a lot of money like my friend, I know that you have a far better chance if you use this simple two-step research process. Please also understand that there are several other superior search tools that you can use as you become more familiar with the process. I will cover them in detail in Chapter 6.

Great Ways to Conduct Product Research

- **Clickbank.com.** This is an excellent place to find what types of products are already selling on the internet. After going to the web site, click on the Buy Products tab and type in the topic you are interested in researching. You will be amazed at the type of information you can obtain here.

- **News Sites.** These usually serve as portals for offline newspaper and broadcasting companies such as CNN (www.CNN.com) and *The New York Times* (www.NYTimes.com). In addition to the latest news stories, you'll find lots of valuable information about the business world, marketplace trends, and the like. Some will even send you automatic e-mail alerts on stories or information containing the keywords that you select.

- **E-zines.** These online magazines offer general as well as more specific information on just about anything; product reviews and assessments; advice and how-to columns; and plenty of feature articles.

- **Chat rooms.** This is a venue for communities of users with similar interests who post messages in real time (like instant messaging).

- **Forums.** These are online discussion groups where participants with common interests can exchange open messages and ideas.

- **Blogs** (short for Web Logs). These sites are publicly accessible personal writing journals that reflect the personality and interests of the site's owner (see Chapters 4 and 11 for more on blogs). These are wonderful tools for discovering more about your prospects' and customers' interests, worries, and opinions. The easiest way to find one that suits your needs is to simply log on to a search engine (e.g., www.google.com or www.msn.com) and type in logical keywords (e.g., "dog blogs" or "dog food blogs" if your site is devoted to gourmet puppy food).

Once you've completed this step, you'll have a much better understanding of your product or service's online possibilities. If you're still stuck, don't give up. Remember, your goal is to uncover a problem that online shoppers have, and offer the best solution for it.

STEP 3: CHOOSE YOUR BEST DELIVERY METHOD

Now that you've done your homework, it's time to fine-tune your offering. Will you sell a product, a service, or both? List your ideas and then decide on the best delivery method. For example, do you want to create a digital product—one that can be downloaded from your web site—or one that necessitates offline delivery? Examples of downloadable digital products include the following:

- MP3 audio files
- e-books (usually in PDF format)
- online forum memberships
- videos

Examples of products or services that cannot be downloaded directly from your web site include:

- CDs
- T-shirts
- hats
- jewelry
- books
- golf lessons
- legal representation
- catering services

As you can see, your choices are almost limitless. That's why you must narrow down your selections by rating them according to how they

- **play to your talents, strengths, skills, and desires.** For instance, if your passion is Persian cats and you're an excellent writer, you might consider developing e-books, e-zines, and newsletters on the care and feeding of the breed. If you can't write well, you might consider selling T-shirts or baseball caps that can be customized with your prospect's favorite cat photos.

- **play to your audience's preferred delivery methods.** Find out what your target audience prefers. For example, are they more likely to read a book, listen to an audio file in their car, or watch an online video?

But wait—what if you're not a skilled writer and your prospects want e-books? Or your audience wants hats and you don't want to warehouse merchandise?

Or they're looking for photographs and you couldn't take a decent picture to save your life? Is all lost? Absolutely not!

You do not have to develop your own products or services. Many successful online marketers sell other people's products exclusively or in addition to their own, via affiliate programs. Although I will go into greater detail in Chapter 10, it's important to note at this point that these programs can be extremely lucrative because you'll earn a percentage of the purchase price (i.e., a commission payment) each time someone buys products or services through your affiliate link. For instance, let's say you offer instructional materials—e-books, CDs, videos—on skiing. In this case,

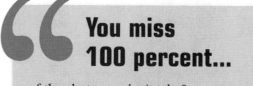

You miss 100 percent...

of the shots you don't take."

—*Wayne Gretzky, retired professional hockey player*

you might also want to sell other companies' skis, jackets, hats, boots, poles, trip packages, and even lift tickets through your site. After all, they are logical extensions of your own product and chances are they appeal to the same target market. (I explain exactly how to sign up for affiliate programs in Chapter 10.)

In the next section I describe what my quiche client decided by using a marketing funnel strategy.

STEP 4: CREATE YOUR PRODUCT LINE USING THE MARKETING FUNNEL APPROACH

Simply said, a marketing funnel strategy is a system that enables you to guide your prospects down a comfortable and logical path leading to the first of many profitable sales. It works for two primary reasons:

1. People buy products and services from companies they know, like, and trust (the relationship).

2. It is much easier and less expensive to sell your products to an existing customer than to acquire a new customer.

Remember, marketing is not a one-shot deal. That's why it's vitally important to plan for the future and have a solid strategy in place.

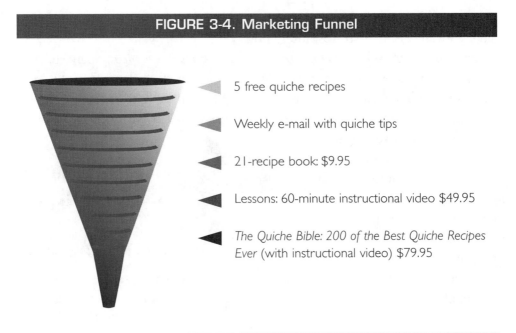

FIGURE 3-4. Marketing Funnel

5 free quiche recipes

Weekly e-mail with quiche tips

21-recipe book: $9.95

Lessons: 60-minute instructional video $49.95

The Quiche Bible: 200 of the Best Quiche Recipes Ever (with instructional video) $79.95

Figure 3-4 illustrates how the quiche entrepreneur used the marketing funnel. As you can see, he first e-mailed five free quiche recipes—one per week for five weeks, using autoresponders (which I discuss in more detail in Chapter 7) to interested prospects who supplied their names and e-mail addresses. Then he followed up with weekly e-mails that included more useful tips on baking the perfect quiche, along with an invitation to purchase his 21-recipe book for $9.95.

Although he was certainly happy to sell the video and quiche bible right away, he recognized that few of his prospects, no matter how much they loved quiche, would be willing to plunk down $49.95, let alone $79.95, right away.

Yet after getting a taste of his exceptional customer service, helpful tips, and delicious quiche recipes, he knew they would be far more likely to want more—and wouldn't mind paying for it.

He was right. His list of involved prospects and customers continued to grow, which translated into more sales and referrals, higher average order amounts, and more frequent purchases. Even better, those highly interested, and targeted, folks helped him create new products that he marketed to them and others!

Here's how: He invited his customers to complete a very short e-mail survey in exchange for five of his newest quiche recipes. Respondents answered questions about the kinds of food and drink they liked to serve with their quiches, and offered suggestions for additional products (e.g., aprons, mixers, specialized flour, teleclasses, one-on-one consulting, etc.) and other types of food recipes they were interested in obtaining.

No matter what your product is,

you are ultimately in the education business. Your customers need to be constantly educated about the many advantages of doing business with you, trained to use your products more effectively, and taught how to make never-ending improvement in their lives."

—*Robert G. Allen,*
author of Multiple Streams of Income

And guess what? He used their ideas to create new products, enter into affiliate agreements with other companies, and add to and repackage his existing line.

REPURPOSING NEW AND EXISTING PRODUCTS AND SERVICES

Repurposing is about using a little bit of energy to obtain a big impact. It's about working smarter, not harder. It's about finding ways to do things more efficiently. It's about taking what you already have and getting the most out of it, like using a tire jack to lift a 3,000 pound automobile, or using low-cost marketing tactics that achieve maximum results. It's getting extra mileage out of new or existing products or services and creating multiple streams of income that complement and augment your core offerings.

HOW DOES THIS WORK IN REAL LIFE?

This concept is best illustrated using the following simple example: Let's say you're a service provider who has created a successful small two-hour business marketing seminar that you present, in person, to chamber of commerce members, SBA work groups, independent small-business owners, and so on. Let's also assume that business is booming—something you'd like to continue—but you're concerned with the amount of effort it is taking you to market your seminar and lack of time you have for your family. Therefore, you're wondering what you can do to keep your business growing and spend more time at home. Here are some ideas:

1. Repackage and repurpose your content

Take your existing product and turn it into five! Here's how:

- Record your seminar and convert it into an audio program on CD or MP3 file for the web.

- Get your seminar transcribed and converted into a workbook, e-book, or online e-course (possibly using online freelancers at www.elance.com).

- Revise your seminar content for other vertical markets (e.g., small-business marketing tips for dentists, physicians, retailers, etc.) and develop additional audio products, workbooks, or e-books.

- Chunk down the seminar content into short tips that you e-mail automatically to your prospect list once a week using autoresponders (see Chapter 7).

2. Bundle your products and services

Package logical items together and offer a price incentive when bought in this manner. (This works particularly well for repeat-purchase consumables.) For example, if you normally offer sales writing e-courses for $29.95 and headline writing software for $19.95, you could package them and sell the bundled product for $39.95. Or what if my quiche client bundled a discounted cooking video with his online cooking class?

Hopefully, by now you're confident of your product or service choices and ready to begin getting your site designed and built.

> **This may seem simple,** but you need to give customers what they want, not what you think they want. And, if you do this, people will keep coming back."
>
> —*John Ilhan, Australian businessman*

WEB WORK: YOUR INTERACTIVE ADVENTURE

1. REMINDER #1

Go to http://inventory.overture.com to learn how many people are searching for your product or service. (I discuss other research tools later in the book.)

2. REMINDER #2

Visit www.google.com to learn more about your competition. Also, make sure to be on the lookout for possible affiliate partners and supplemental products and/or services.

3. CHOOSE A PRODUCT OR SERVICE TO SELL

Use the following template to help guide your thought process. I've also provided a simple example of how one might look. You can download more templates from my web site at www.OnlineMarketingTemplates.com.

My Passions	My Strengths, Skills, and Talents	My Resources and Ideal Business Model	Types of Products That Make Use of These Strengths and Resources
I love teaching small children new things	1. Able to summarize information in easy-to-understand steps 2. Good written and oral skills 3. Knowledge of innovative potty-training method	1. Very little money—do not want to buy or inventory materials 2. Have full-time job so want business that can be put on autopilot for most part	Instructional material on how to potty train toddlers 1. Downloadable e-book 2. Mini e-course 3. Online audios 4. Online videos

Now it's your turn...

My Passions	My Strengths, Skills, and Talents	My Resources and Ideal Business Model	Types of Products That Make Use of These Strengths and Resources

4. REPURPOSE YOUR EXISTING RESOURCES

In the space below, identify areas you are not repurposing and specific things you could do to get more mileage out of them.

_____

_____

_____

_____

5. CREATE YOUR MARKETING FUNNEL

Decide what your goals are (e.g., lead generation or product sales). Be specific about the types of products you can make and sell, then develop your own product and service marketing funnel.

CHAPTER 3 REMINDERS

Before moving on to Chapter 4: "Design and Navigation: The Key to Making Your Web Site Dynamic and Visitor Friendly," let's take a minute to review the most important lessons learned from this chapter:

- Begin your product or service selection with passion; don't chase opportunity.

- Do your homework. Make sure people want, and are actively seeking, what you'll be selling.

- Leverage your products and services for maximum profits.

- Visit my web site if you'd like to learn more; you'll find free up-to-the-minute blogs, advice, articles, templates, and resources. Go to www.MasteringOnlineMarketing.com.

> " **The average person has four ideas a year** which, if any one is acted on, would make them a millionaire."
>
> —*Brian Tracy, author and motivational speaker*

DESIGN AND NAVIGATION

Making Your Web Site Dynamic and Visitor Friendly

In this chapter you'll learn

- *essential steps for planning your web site's design and usability*

- *why your site's design can either make or break your e-commerce business*

- *why blogs are great alternatives to traditional web sites*

- *five rules for creating a professional-looking web site*

...and much more.

> ## " I don't start with a design objective...
>
> I start with a communication objective. I feel my project is successful if it communicates what it is supposed to communicate."
>
> —*Mike Davidson, founder and CEO of Newsvine.com*

Would you go back to a restaurant where the tables were dirty and the floors were covered with leftover food? Would you enter a shoe store that had old, worn-out shoes in the display window? Would you buy advice on organizing your closets from someone with a cluttered office?

As with these traditional business examples, your web site's appearance and ease of navigation are a direct reflection of you, your company, and your products and can literally make or break your business. And it takes online visitors an average of just seconds to decide whether they like the look and feel of your site and if they can begin to trust you as a credible resource. If they do, you're over the first hump. If not, it's all over. They won't be back. That's why it's vitally important that you do everything in your power to ensure that your web site is *welcoming* and *easy to read and use*.

Sounds easy enough, doesn't it? Sure. I mean, how hard can it be? Not awfully. But that's just the problem. It's fairly simple to create a web site and just about anybody can do it. So many entrepreneurs do just that: They slap something up without giving it much thought, and it shows. Their web sites are filled with irksome animations, tiny print, and garish colors. They have links that go nowhere and their visitors leave—overwhelmed, confused, and/or irritated.

Even worse, these entrepreneurs don't succeed in building mailing lists, developing relationships, or making money. These are really nice people with cool online products and they go out of business and wonder what went wrong. Although there are lots of other reasons that this happens, one thing is clear. Many online businesses go bust because their owners underestimate the importance of learning and adhering to essential web development, design, and navigation principles. This is an extremely common, and lethal, mistake.

I don't want this to happen to you, so please pay very close attention to the advice and tips I provide in this chapter. They are the most important basics for building, or improving, your web site's appearance and usability.

Learn them. Use them. Do not rely on luck or good old horse sense. Do not fool yourself into thinking anyone can do this stuff and that it's no big deal. Do not invite anyone to your site until you are absolutely, positively, 100 percent sure that your visitors' experience will be delightful.

Let's begin with some fundamentals.

THE BASICS

It is possible to build a site that meets your needs, wows your visitors, and doesn't cost a fortune, but only if you plan ahead. Although this may seem apparent, more often than not, this approach is ignored in favor of getting something up fast. When online marketing is approached in this hasty manner, the result is a web site that is cumbersome, unattractive, amateurish, and/or very expensive. So before beginning, take some time to plan your site. It's not as hard as you may think, and you'll be glad you did.

Before we begin, however, a reminder: By now you should already know:

- your target audience: who they are and where to find them
- the products or services you'll offer and their main benefits
- your niche
- why doing business with you is smart.

Now let's start building your plan.

STEP 1: DEFINE YOUR WEB SITE'S PRIMARY GOAL

Although there are web sites that provide free information, trouble-shooting advice, after-sale customer support, entertainment, and the like, I'll focus on ones devoted to e-commerce (lead generation and sales). E-commerce sites can be one page, or many, and the form you choose will depend upon your short- and long-term objectives. Simply said, the ultimate goal is profitable sales. However, based on many different factors your web site may serve as a vehicle for capturing leads for future sales—online or offline.

Here are the four basic types of web sites:

1. **Sales Only.** These web sites are dedicated to one thing only: furthering and closing product and/or service sales. Period.

2. **Lead Generation: List Building for Future Online Sales.** These web sites are devoted to motivating future online sales. Generally they offer free information (e.g., articles, reports, mini courses, etc.) for visitors who elect to opt in (i.e., provide their name and e-mail address) and often move their prospects through a marketing funnel (explained in Chapter 3.)

3. **Lead Generation for Future Offline Sales.** These web sites are designed to encourage future offline sales. They usually provide information about their products and/or services, directions to their location (if applicable), answers to frequently asked questions, contact information, and the like. These are the types of sites that service professionals find most useful.

4. **Lead Generation for Future Online and/or Offline Sales.** Sometimes online marketers—particularly those with multiple products and services—use their web sites to gather prospect leads for their online and offline businesses.

STEP 2: CHOOSE THE TYPE OF WEB SITE THAT WILL HELP YOU ACHIEVE YOUR GOAL

Once you've defined the type of site you need, it's time to select the level of complexity that will work best. There are six to choose from:

1. Dedicated Sales Page

This is a direct-marketing (with compelling offer and strong call to action) web site, focused on closing online sales. Although it may have multiple pages (e.g., Frequently Asked Questions, Testimonials, About Us, etc.) it usually consists of a strong sales letter that leads to a shopping cart or PayPal link (see Figure 4-1).

2. Single Opt-In Page

Also called a squeeze page, this is a one-page web site designed to limit its visitors' choices. Users are invited to take action—most often to opt in (provide their name and e-mail address in exchange for an offer)—or leave. The copy usually consists of a headline, a bulleted list of benefits, graphics, testimonials, a strong call to action, and an opt-in link.

3. Membership Sites

Membership web sites are usually very content driven and highly focused on a specific niche or subject area. Most often, paying subscribers are granted

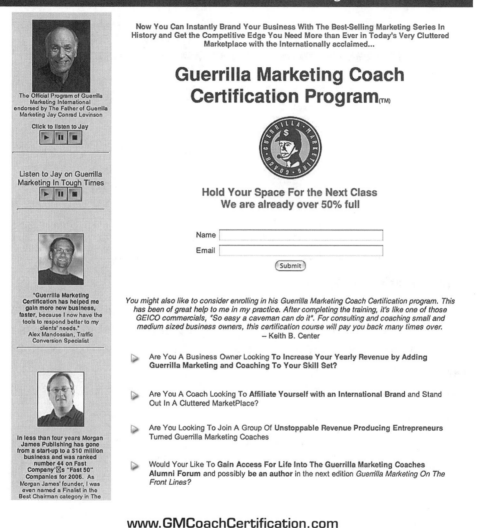

FIGURE 4-1. Dedicated Sales Page

access to exclusive documents, forums, downloads, and the like (although many sites do not charge for these services). Figure 4-2 shows a screenshot of www.InternetTips.com, an example of a nicely designed, well-written, and content-driven membership site.

FIGURE 4-2. Membership Web Site

www.InternetTips.com

4. Information or Brochure Web Sites

Like their names suggest, these web sites function similarly to traditional brochures. They provide information about a company and its products and services in hopes of stimulating offline sales. They usually consist of multiple pages, such as a:

- home page
- contact us
- frequently asked questions
- our products/services, and
- testimonials.

5. Blogs

Personalized journal web sites, or blogs, contain a series of interactive and sequential posts (messages centered around specific topics) authored by the site's owner and visitors. They are wonderful tools for creating a quick online presence (you can have one up and running in minutes), sharing ideas (most offer RSS or ATOM syndication feeds so people can subscribe and receive

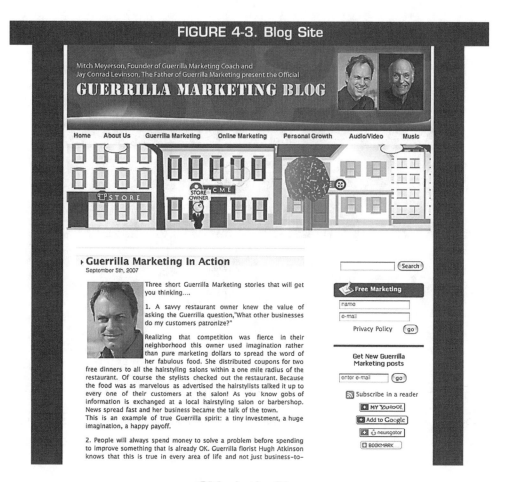

FIGURE 4-3. Blog Site

www.GMarketingBlog.com

updated posts), showcasing audio and video clips, and much more. An ever-growing number of online marketers are using blogs to replace more traditional e-commerce web sites. Figure 4-3 is a good example of a blog site.

6. Portal Sites

Most often portal web sites serve as main hubs, by providing direct links to their owners', or others', sites or web pages. Many marketers use them to begin their visitors' online journey, particularly when they offer multiple

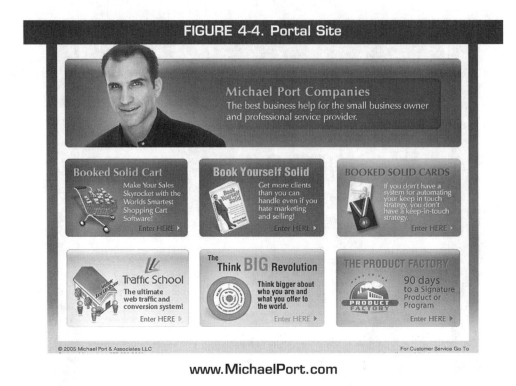

FIGURE 4-4. Portal Site

www.MichaelPort.com

products on more than one web site. Some portal web sites have shopping carts; others are purely informational. Figure 4-4 contains a great example of an e-commerce portal site.

STEP 3: SELECT AND REGISTER YOUR DOMAIN NAME

A domain name is your business's identity and it's how people will find your web pages. Just as there are multiple roads leading to the same location, one or many domain names can point to identical web sites and/or pages.

Before choosing a name, remember to keep in mind your target audiences' personalities and what they're hoping to find on your site, your product or service offerings, and what specifically you'd like your visitors to do. *Why?* Because it's best to pick a domain name that defines your business and its purpose. Also, if your goal is to create a long- term online business, then you'll want to pick a name that effectively *brands* you and that you'll feel comfortable using on one or more sites. You should even consider buying your own, or your company's, name.

Conversely, you may choose a more generic domain name that describes what you do or offer and includes important keywords. But don't go overboard, otherwise your domain name may end up being too long, making it hard to remember and even harder to spell, and it will get cut off in e-mails— a no-no (e.g., www.small-business-strategic-marketing-e-books.com). Use your imagination to come up with shorter terms and abbreviations that will be just as effective (e.g., www.smaic.com for www.strategicmarketingadvisors.com).

Your domain name should be

■ short and sweet

■ memorable

■ descriptive (i.e., include important keywords)

■ easy to explain, speak (especially over the phone), spell, and print (even on a small business card)

■ dot-com. Try to find a domain name with a ".com" extension instead of .net, .biz, .org, etc. Many people assume that all URLs end in .com and may not look any further if they can't find your site right away.

Registering your Domain Name

I'm shocked at the numbers of online marketers who are still paying $20 or more per month to register their domain names with search engines. This is completely unnecessary.

Go to a reputable company such as Godaddy.com or www.1and1.com for very low rates or log on to my web site (www.OnlineMarketingSuperstore.com) if you'd like more information or resources for registering your domain name.

I'm often asked if buying multiple domain names is a good idea, and my answer is always a definite usually. While I'm not a fan of people or companies who buy lots of domain names solely to prevent others from using them, I do think it's a good idea to think ahead about your future needs; otherwise it may be too late when you want to buy another name. In addition to the instances I cited above, you should consider purchasing multiple domain names if it will prevent your competitors from purchasing one too similar to yours, and if using both a generic and branding name would help get visitors to your site.

STEP 4: CHOOSE A COMPANY TO HOST YOUR SITE

First, in order to select the right host for your site, find out what tools and services it supports and which ones it doesn't. There are lots of choices on the internet but my favorite is www.SuperstarHostingAndDomains.com, because you'll get a lot for your money. In any event, choose a hosting company that

- **includes measurement tools.** More and more companies are bundling potent web analytics technology into their standard hosting packages. Since tracking and analyzing conversions and traffic is extremely important (I discuss this in greater detail in Chapter 6), find out what your prospective hosts offer. It's usually easier and more cost-effective to get your software set up earlier rather than later.

- **is tough on spammers.** Given today's internet environment, this should not be a consideration, it should be a requirement. Since you'll be sending and receiving e-mails via your host's servers, make sure they have safeguards in place so spammers can't use them to jump-start their campaigns. Fortunately (or unfortunately, depending on your perspective), ISPs (internet service providers) regularly blocklist (also referred to as blacklist) and/or penalize hosting companies that fail to police these activities carefully. So if you're not a spammer, why be concerned? Because most, or all, of the e-mails that originate from your host company's servers—including yours—will be blocked, and worse, you won't even know it happened. The good news is you can find out if the company you're considering is blocklisted before you make a decision by going to www.spamhaus.org.

- **is reliable.** No matter how carefully you select a hosting company, you'll still experience cyberspace glitches—times when your site will be down or slow for short periods. However, for some hosting companies these snafus occur often and may last many hours or even days. That's a big problem. In addition to the obvious hit to your wallet, it will also frustrate would-be visitors to your site, at least temporarily.

It's a good idea to find out how the companies you're considering fare in the service performance department. And since most claim that their servers are 99 percent reliable—and we know they're not—consult a more objective source. A good way to find out is to conduct a little search engine research; they have past and current data on hosts' reliability records.

If your web site is your only source of income or represents a major business investment, you should definitely consider dedicated hosting. It's more expensive, but since your site will be placed on its own individual server, it's far more reliable.

One last tip: Avoid using free hosting. You'll have a harder time finding people who are willing to link to your site and the banner ads the host will place on your page may turn off your visitors.

STEP 5: CHOOSE A SITE BUILDER, TEMPLATE, OR BLOG

Selecting your site builder is another big consideration, which many entrepreneurs erroneously approach with a short-term perspective. Please think very carefully before hiring the college kid next door or a friend of a friend to build your site. Why? Because best cost is not always least cost, and this is one of those times when you almost always get exactly what you pay for. The last thing you need is a site that's slow, unreliable, hard to use, and/or

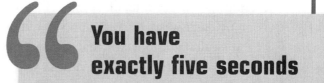

You have exactly five seconds
to make your intentions known."
—*Maria Veloso, copywriting expert*

antagonistic to search engines. This doesn't mean, however, that you should pay a fortune. If you're smart, you'll look for a high-quality freelancer who will build your site very reasonably.

Before beginning this process, remember that speed, dependability, usability (navigation), surfability (search engine optimization), and professional design are your most critical considerations. If your site lacks even one of these features, you will have a much harder time getting traffic and converting prospects into customers. So go online and search. Look for sites—preferably ones outside of your industry—that look and act as you envision your own. When you find one, jot down the web developer's name and contact information (usually located at the bottom of the home page) and then call or e-mail the site's owner (they are usually willing to supply you with the web developer's information if you can't locate it online). Ask him questions such as:

- Are you happy with the design, functionality, and reliability of your site?
- Are you pleased with your web developer's level of expertise, project execution, and ongoing customer support services?
- What types of services does this company provide (e.g., graphic design)?
- What does the company do best? Worst?
- How often does the developer perform system maintenance?

Then, come up with a realistic budget based on your available money, minimum site requirements, and ideal add-ons. If, after obtaining at least three quotes from reputable developers, you're way over budget—it's time to cut costs. Start by getting rid of any extras; those features that would be nice to have but are not critical, such as Flash animations. Also, ask your developer for other money-saving tips and what, if any, features could be easily added later on.

It is vitally important that your site be maintained and updated often, or your credibility and effectiveness will go down the tubes. And since learning how to use a web-authoring program is easier than ever, there is simply no good reason to hand control over to anyone else (and you'll save money as well!).

With today's easy-to-use technology, there's no reason to rely on a web developer every time you want to make content changes on the fly. The good news is that it's easier than you may have expected. In fact, most web-authoring programs like Adobe Dreamweaver, Contribute, Microsoft FrontPage, and free open source CMS (content managing system) such as Joomla are very much like Microsoft Word. They'll help you truly take control of your web site without breaking a sweat.

Blogs

There is something you can do that I strongly advise you to consider, particularly if you're strapped for money and/or pressed for time. More and more online entrepreneurs and business owners are wisely using blogs (combination of two words—"web" and "log") to support or replace more formalized web sites. Commonly used for personal journaling, blog owners start a conversation and invite visitors to comment. But don't mistake these sites for glorified diaries; blogs are taking on a whole new life as exceptional e-commerce tools for many reasons.

First, they can generate more income if they're used as an extension of your current marketing efforts. They can help you establish yourself as an industry expert, gain more visibility and media attention, and increase your qualified leads. Additionally, there are many people who now earn thousands of dollars each month blogging about topics they love. The key to their success is based on three things:

> ## "The foundation for successful blogging
>
> comes down to three simple words: passion, publish, profit. Find something you love and start to write about it… often. Then see where the search engines take you."
>
> —*Andy Wibbels, author of* BlogWild
> *(www.andywibbels.com)*

1. **Readers.** Online surfers looking for specific information are often referred to blogs by search engines.

2. **Content.** Once there, the visitors read conversations that discuss the information they requested.

3. **Advertising.** In addition to content, visitors see ads for products related to their interests.

Blogs are managed by software (called blog platforms) that run on a web site's server. That means there's nothing to install or download and they can be accessed through any browser. Some popular blog platforms can be found at www.Blogger.com, www.TypePad.com, and www.WordPress.com.

Here's why blogs make such great sense for entrepreneurs:

■ **Hosting costs little or nothing.** There are many good, reputable companies who will host your blog for a small fee or absolutely free (my favorite is www.WordPress.com).

■ **You'll save time.** Your site can literally be up and running in a matter of minutes and you won't waste time going through a web developer every time you want to make a change.

■ **You'll save money and look professional.** You can use your host's design templates, which will ensure that your site looks great without having to pay a web designer.

■ **The search engines love them.** Because a blog's pages are frequently updated and are interlinked with other web sites, they often rank higher in search results.

■ **They're extremely versatile and can be used for almost any purpose.** Blogs are also more spontaneous than other web sites and actively encourage interaction between web site owners and visitors.

■ **They can be published in multiple formats.** Because they're stored in a database, you can easily add video, audio, graphics, shopping carts, photos, RSS feeds, PDF files, and so on. Even better, blogs can be viewed on multiple portable devices such as cell phones, iPods, MP3 players, and the like.

In my opinion the only two reasons for not considering a blog are if you don't like to write—even informally (remember the entries are more like e-mails than stricter copywriting)—or you're unwilling or unable to update your blog every 24 to 48 hours.

To get a better sense of the variety of blogs on the internet, visit sites such as www.Technorati.com, www.IceRocket.com, and www.BlogPulse.com and use their search features to find ones on your favorite subjects.

STEP 6: DESIGN A PROFESSIONAL-LOOKING SITE

As I said before, your web site is your company's face and a direct reflection of you, your business, and your products and services. If your visitors like what they see, they'll stay longer; if they don't, they'll leave—and they'll make this decision in seconds. Simply said, first-rate design is critical for your online success, even though it's sometimes difficult to achieve. That's why you must approach this step wisely and thoughtfully.

> "Success leaves clues."
>
> —Anthony Robbins, American life coach, writer, and professional speaker

There are three basic components of design: *Typeface* (how your text *looks*—color, size, fonts—not to be confused with *what* you say, which I cover in Chapter 5); *graphics* (pictures, drawings, buttons, backgrounds, etc.), and *links* (connections to other pages or sites). Your visitors will notice these elements first and search engines will rate you on them (among other things). Your web site must look and feel professional, pleasant, welcoming, and easy to read and use (which I cover in the next section)—a tall order. Since individual tastes vary widely, where do you begin and how will you know if and when your site is well designed?

Simple. First, there are thousands of well-designed web sites, so start there. Why reinvent the wheel? I'm not suggesting that you plagiarize, I am advising you to take the best elements from several different sites and make them your own.

After you've come up with your best ideas, write them down and sketch a rough draft of your vision on paper (or use software like Adobe Photoshop or even Microsoft PowerPoint). Once you've completed your sketch, decide who will create the final design: you alone, you with some help, or a professional designer. If you're not a trained graphic designer and/or not completely confident of your ability to design a professional-looking site, you should not do this alone. Trust me, you won't be happy with the finished product.

Alternatively, you can create a superbly designed site with help, specifically by purchasing a template. They're extremely affordable, flexible, and for the most part, great looking. You'll find lots of online companies offering these products; www.LuckyMarble.com and www.TemplateMonster.com are two of my favorites. I do not recommend this option for beginners, even though the finished product looks great and it's far less expensive than hiring a professional designer. If you go this route, you'll need to purchase web site editing software such as Dreamweaver or GoLive (both from Adobe) or Microsoft's FrontPage and download an FTP (file transfer protocol) program. Then, after you've figured out how to use them—a time-consuming process—the real fun begins. You'll create, save, refine, save, upload, change, save, view, yell, save, and upload... over and over again.

If you don't have the money to hire someone and/or don't have the skill to work with templates, your best bet is a blog (covered in the previous section).

FIVE RULES FOR DESIGNING YOUR SITE

Now that you understand the steps involved in getting your web site up, it's time to learn what you need to know, and do, to ensure that it makes the cut. Following are five rules that you can use to create a well-designed site.

RULE #1: Learn and Apply Basic Principles of Color and Layout

Unlike printed copy, web site design comes with its own set of unique challenges. After all, your visitors are not seeing words, photos, colors, and graphics on paper, they're viewing them on a computer monitor, iPod, or even a cell phone. So, in addition to utilizing many of the same time-tested design elements that apply to print documents, you'll also have to adjust some elements for the internet. Here are some quick tips for making the most of color and layout:

- Use color carefully and limit the number you use. Don't visually assault your visitors by using lots of loud colors that jump off the page.

- Lay out your page so that the most important information is the most visible (e.g., headlines, benefit statements, etc.).

- Use fonts that are readable. Tiny text may look cool to you, but it can be very irritating to those without perfect vision. And while most sites allow the visitor to enlarge the text, others do not (especially Flash sites). Also, don't make your visitors struggle to read typefaces that are too fancy.

■ Aim for consistency. All of your pages should have a similar look and navigation system.

■ Keep it simple. Don't use nonstop, nerve-rattling Flash animations (they're expensive and annoying and will slow downloading time) and/or embossed-bordered rules and tables.

RULE #2: Make Speed a Priority

Your site should load quickly. If it takes more than ten seconds to load (even with a 56K modem), your visitors will click away, hoping to find the products they seek elsewhere. Here are some quick tips to ensure that your pages load quickly:

■ Keep your file sizes small. The bigger they are, the longer they'll take to load.

■ Use few images and minimize their quality (compress them).

■ Avoid large—or too many—banners and/or graphics.

■ Use Flash animation (or other special effects) sparingly and only if it adds a "wow" element. Do not use it as an entry page to your site.

RULE #3: Adjust Your Settings to Accommodate
Different Browsers and Computer Monitors

Keep in mind that your visitors will view your site under a variety of situations and on various devices. They will be viewing your web pages on Macintosh computers, PCs, small screens, large monitors, as well as via multiple browsers. Each of these variables will affect the way people see your page. Therefore, consult with your web developer to ensure that your site is optimized for different users' experiences. Then check how it looks on different browsers by visiting www.anybrowser.com or by downloading several onto your computer (e.g., Internet Explorer, FireFox, Mozilla, and Netscape).

Without going into unnecessary detail, the simplest thing to do is to make sure that your site complies with the world wide web's established W3C

Your Computer Screen Isn't a Magazine

you take to the bathroom. A full 79% of internet users SCAN the page. It's true. We've turned into human browsers! Reading on the web is a completely different experience from reading a paperback on your nightstand or the newspaper on the Stairmaster. Your copy MUST be scannable. Here are three key methods to make readers gobble up your web message online:

1. Highlight your keywords. Use different colors, bold, italics, or all caps, but make those keywords stand out. This is particularly hard to do with plain text e-zines, huh?

2. Use meaningful headlines and sub-heads. Don't waste your web real estate on clever phrases. Your prospects read the headline first, then decide if they'll take the time to read any further.

3. Use lots of white space. You can guide their eyes where you want them to go, if you have a path for them. Don't clutter up the page with too many confusing options.

What does all this mean to you? It means if you want your web copy to be read, you'd better develop a strategy of words that's friendly to the eye.

—Lorrie Morgan-Ferrero (www.Red-Hot-Copy.com)

(WWW Consortium) standards. If you'd like to learn more about this process, visit www.w3.org.

RULE #4: Use Internet Design Standards to Make Your Site Easy to Navigate and Use

If you're like me, you've abandoned many web sites long before you got to the shopping cart page because it just wasn't worth the effort. It's the same as when you walk into a store and then turn around and walk right back out because whatever you want isn't worth what you'd have to go through to get it.

Here's a simple analogy: Let's say you are pressed for time but need to replace your broken coffee maker carafe. Since you know exactly the type you need, have cash in hand, and there's a Wal-Mart on your way, you decide to pop in and make a quick purchase, figuring it should take no longer than ten minutes, tops.

However, things don't quite work out the way you planned. You're greeted by long checkout lines and slow cashiers, crowded aisles, confusing signage, employees who send you to the wrong department, and finally, boxes of coffee carafes that are not priced and can't be reached with a ladder. Will you stay and endure, or go?

The answer depends on many things, such as how badly you want or need the product and what other options you have. In this example, it's difficult to bail because you've already invested a great deal of your time and you'd end up wasting even more trying to find another place that sells coffee carafes.

This is not the case for internet shoppers. If you don't connect with people and make it easy for them to do what you'd like, they will go somewhere else—instantly. Therefore, your site's navigation must be clear, simple, and standard. If you want your visitors to feel comfortable, design your site to accommodate what they've come to expect. In other words, place commonly used elements where people expect to find them. There's plenty of ways to make your site stand out from the rest, but deviating from the norm in this instance is not a good idea. Here are some quick tips you can use right away:

- Use standard underlined blue text to signify a live link (hyperlink) to another site or page.

- If visitor identification is required to use your site, this should be accomplished via user name and password verifications.

- Unless specified otherwise, all live links should lead to an HTML document

- Online purchases should be placed in a shopping cart that leads to a virtual checkout process.

- Position subordinate or miscellaneous page menus or links at the bottom of the page.

- Include a site map that links to and from your home page and all other major pages on your site.

- Make sure that all your links are working, otherwise you'll frustrate your visitors and irritate the search engines.

- Make it easy for your visitors to bookmark your page. Use a gentle reminder and/or a *favicon* (a small logo that's automatically picked up and displayed in your visitors' "favorites" explorer bar).

RULE #5: Understand that Web Design Differs from Web Development

Without going into too much detail, it's important to realize that there is a difference between web design (how the site looks and functions) and web development (the technical elements and coding). In fact, your final site and its ultimate effectiveness are heavily influenced by its under-the-hood infrastructure—that hidden world of HTML coding and Java scripting.

However, don't worry about understanding it all. Just be aware that what's in place behind the scenes will impact your visitors' experience and your success on the internet. Leave the details to your web developer, but make sure he or she is knowledgeable and skilled in applying the latest techniques. For example, CSS (cascading style sheet) technology now allows designers to quickly transform an entire web site by making changes on one page. It also prevents your web pages from looking ragged and helps reduce the time it takes to load each page.

> # The details are not in the details.
>
> They make the design."
>
> —*Charles Eames, American designer*

And you've probably heard, but may not completely understand, the term "HTML coding." If so, don't worry. All you need to know is that HTML, or hypertext markup language, is one of the coding languages that web developers use to create internet documents. Fortunately, today's web sites are designed using a much friendlier word processing version, such as Microsoft's WYSIWYG (What-You-See-Is-What-You-Get).

WEB WORK: YOUR INTERACTIVE ADVENTURE

1. IF YOU HAVEN'T BUILT YOUR WEB SITE YET

Use the checklist in Figure 4-5 to help guide your planning process.

FIGURE 4-5. Web Site Planning Checklist

My web site's primary goal is:

❑ direct/immediate online sales only

❑ lead generation: list building for future online sales

❑ lead generation for future offline sales

❑ lead generation for future online and/or offline sales

The type of web site I will use to help me achieve these goals is:

❑ a dedicated sales page

❑ a single opt-in page

❑ a membership site

❑ an information or brochure web site

❑ a blog

❑ a portal site

The domain name(s) that I've chosen for my web site:

_____

_____

_____

_____

My web site will be hosted by _____

I will use the following resources to help build my web site (fill in specific companies):

❑ Web developer _____

❑ Graphic designer _____

❑ Copywriter _____

❑ Design template _____

❑ Blog template _____

2. IF YOUR SITE IS ALREADY UP

Use the checklist in Figure 4-6 to ensure that your web site is well designed and easy to use.

FIGURE 4-6. Design and Navigation Checklist

My web site's:

❑ Pages load quickly

❑ Fonts are easy to read

❑ Background colors are muted for easy reading

❑ Look and feel are consistent on each page

❑ Most important information is also the most visible

❑ Special features—Flash animation, graphics, and banners—are used carefully and tastefully

❑ Settings are configured to accommodate different browsers and computer monitors

❑ Directions and navigation are clear, simple, and logical

❑ Internal and external links are working properly

❑ Site map is clearly marked on my home page

❑ Visitors are encouraged to bookmark my pages

❑ Primary page menus are across the top of the page

3. FINDING A DOMAIN NAME

Good domain names are not as easy to come by as they used to be, so if you're having trouble finding one, or narrowing down your selection, try one or both of the following:

- **Choose five to ten domain names that you like**—some short and some longer (shorter ones are usually harder to get). It's also a good idea to try them out on several people before choosing one.

■ **Go to www.OnlineMarketingSuperstore.com** to see if your chosen name is still available. If so, register it there or elsewhere. By the way, if your first choices are not available, sites like this one will provide you with a list of alternatives to choose from.

CHAPTER 4 REMINDERS

Before moving on to Chapter 5, "Dynamic Web Copy: The Key to Getting People to Respond," let's take a minute to review the most important lessons learned from this chapter:

■ You have only one chance to make a good first impression.

■ Don't underestimate the importance of great design and friendly navigation.

■ Make sure your web designer fully understands web coding and infrastructure.

■ Remember to make speed a priority when designing your web site.

> **" A merchant who approaches business** with the idea of serving the public well has nothing to fear from the competition."
>
> *—James Cash Penney, founder of JCPenney Corporation*

DYNAMIC WEB COPY

The Key to Getting People to Respond

In this chapter you'll learn

- *how to use direct response communication to achieve your e-commerce goals*

- *the most important things to do before writing your own sales copy*

- *how to use essential copywriting elements*

- *simple but powerful language tips*

...and much more.

> " **Make it simple.**
> **Make it memorable.**
> Make it inviting to look at. Make it fun to read."
>
> —*Leo Burnett, legendary advertising executive*

It doesn't matter if you're big or small. It doesn't matter if you have a tiny budget or deep pockets. It doesn't matter if you want to increase your market share; demonstrate your expertise; offer packaged goods for direct sale; build an e-mail list; educate prospects on your service offerings; ease order-desk inquiries; encourage brick-and-mortar sales; or sell information.

> ## Either write something worth reading...
> or do something worth writing."
>
> —*Benjamin Franklin*

If you don't create and deliver a clear, well-thought-out, and relevant promotional message, your site will fail. And since the quality of your product is without question (I hope) your challenge is how to effectively communicate with your targeted prospects so you can get and keep profitable customers as quickly as possible. This is particularly important today because of other big barriers to e-commerce success, such as the tremendously high level of white noise, clutter, and fierce competition on the internet; the public's belief that there isn't anything new of real value there; and the impersonal nature of cyberspace. You've got an uphill battle.

In order to overcome these somewhat daunting challenges, you must first understand how vitally important it is for you to become an excellent communicator. Why? Because

- people do business with people they know, like, and trust
- people know, like, and trust people who respect their intelligence and take time to develop lasting connections
- people are more likely to develop lasting connections with people who communicate effectively.

Since you're building an e-commerce site that will offer exceptional products, you must be able to effectively converse with your prospects and customers and talk to them using language that is relevant and comfortable. This is the way great relationships begin—even though it is easier to say than to achieve. (But that's good, or everyone would be doing it.) In this chapter I provide you with the strategies, tools, tactics, and know-how necessary to create superior e-commerce sales letters.

SALES LETTER OVERVIEW

Simply said, your sales letter is a form of direct-response communication—a tool to help you achieve your objectives. It is basically a conversation between a person or company and its products' intended end users. It contains a clear and direct offer and an invitation to act (e.g., phone call, location visit, newsletter sign-up, e-mail address, immediate sale, etc.). Unlike more traditional forms of advertising, like branding, customer actions can and should be tracked, measured, and analyzed.

THINGS YOU MUST KNOW BEFORE BEGINNING

Before you can begin writing an effective sales letter, you should already be very clear on the following:

- Product or service selection—what you'll offer for sale
- Marketing funnel approach—or your sales process (the number and types of action steps you'll invite your visitors to take)
- Type of web site—lead generation, sales, etc.
- Product or service's unique selling proposition and key benefits—why you've got the best solution for your target audience's most pressing problems
- Target audience—those who are actively seeking your products or services

THE MOST IMPORTANT THINGS TO DO BEFORE WRITING YOUR OWN SALES COPY

As I discussed in the last chapter, people surf the web looking for specific information. When they land on a sales page, they scan it quickly to see if anything catches their interest. You've already learned the important role that design and navigation plays in keeping them there; now it's time to delve into the words.

Unfortunately many schools today pay little attention to teaching excellent writing skills, making it difficult for many of us to express ourselves effectively. Some of us use 15 words when 4 would do just fine. Some of us are terrible spellers. Some of us don't know the difference between a noun and a verb, let alone a dangling participle. Some of us mix tenses (heaven forbid) in the middle of a sentence. And some of us don't know where to begin.

> ## If I had more time,
>
> I would have written a shorter letter."
>
> —*Blaise Pascal,*
> *French mathematician and philosopher*

That's why your first task is to candidly evaluate your own writing skills. Ask yourself where you fit, and be ruthlessly honest—the success of your web site depends upon it. For instance, are you someone who finds it difficult to express your thoughts in writing? Do you dread writing anything—even a grocery list? Or do you enjoy writing but find that you're often misunderstood?

It may not be comfortable or easy to rate yourself, but do so anyway. You may be remarkably unaware of your communication strengths and weaknesses and this lack of knowledge may be sabotaging your business efforts more than you know. If you're having difficulty assessing your skills, write something and ask friends, family members, and/or co-workers to give you honest feedback.

If you find that your skills are lacking, please get help. Even though you know your products, services, prospects, customers, and company better than anyone and should oversee all of your marketing efforts, leave the writing to experts. Write down what you want to say—your offer, benefits, pricing information, and the like—then let a professional craft the message for you. I strongly advise you to hire a freelance copywriter. They are affordable and worth their weight in gold. If you really can't afford one, find a skilled friend or family member to help you. In either case, make sure you edit, edit, edit.

SALES LETTER LENGTH—LONG OR SHORT?

I'm often asked to advise people on whether their online sales letter should be short or long. During the last several years the trend has been toward long letters, but recently the debate has heated up again and there seems to be no definitive answer other than this: Your sales letter should be as long as it needs to be.

Clear as mud? Well, here it is another way. Your sales letter should contain all of the information your prospects need to decide whether they want to continue the conversation. As long as your content is relevant and informative to *them*, not *you*, it should stay.

As soon as you've finished writing your sales letter—whether long or short—do one more thing: go through it and eliminate any unnecessary words. Get rid of anything that doesn't bring your prospects one step closer to completing the requested action.

SUMMARIZE USING UNDERSTANDABLE HEADINGS AND TITLES

Web visitors are looking for easy-to-follow and logically ordered text. The more you understand this, the better your copy will be. Following is a basic outline of how it should be structured. (You may be surprised to see how much it resembles a term paper outline!)

Part 1: The Headline (and subheads as appropriate)

Part 2: The Introduction—welcome, opening statement

Part 3: The Statement of Facts—bullet points with your products' most compelling benefits

Part 4: The Discussion—why your prospects should listen; your story and/or why you're the best person to solve their problems (your promise)

Part 5: The Proof—objective facts that back up your claims

Part 6: Risk and Roadblock Reversals–ironclad guarantee, payment plans, risk-free trial, and so on

Part 7: The Conclusion—summary of key points, repetition, call to action, postscript

Although I'm going to mix these elements up a bit, this outline is a good tool to use for organizing your thoughts. Now your challenge will be to blend the parts seamlessly together so your entire message appears effortless and intuitive.

COPYWRITING STYLE BASICS

In order to construct a hard-hitting sales letter for your e-commerce site you'll need to begin with a winning business and marketing mindset, and craft a letter that begins to build sustainable relationships.

To that end, your sales letter must convey your genuine concern for your prospects' most pressing problems. In the last chapter you learned how to enhance the look and feel of your site, make it simple to use, and select easy-to-read typefaces. However, now that you're preparing to communicate, it's vitally important to understand that the tone of your words is as important as the words themselves. In other words, you'll need to decide what to say as well as how you'll say it—which is referred to as *style*. Following is a list of six style rules that will help you develop your web copy, regardless of your product or service, industry, or company size.

> ## I don't know the rules of grammar...
>
> If you're trying to persuade people to do something, or buy something, it seems to me you should use their language, the language they use every day, the language in which they think. We try to write in the vernacular."
>
> —*David Ogilvy, American advertising legend*

Rule 1: Write as You Talk and Talk at Your Prospects' Level

I strongly recommend that all web copy be written informally and in a manner that reflects your personality and, more importantly, that of your targeted audience. Also, it's important to connect with your prospects and customers on a human level, so don't be afraid to show some warts (most people are suspicious of perfection anyway). Moreover, stay humble. Use short sentences with clear and simple language. If your readers have to consult a dictionary just to understand you, you're in big trouble.

Rule 2: Don't Mistake Informal with Sloppy

Casually conversing with your prospects, as you would a friend, is great; being careless is not. Don't let your credibility suffer because of punctuation errors, poor use of language, and misspellings. Here are some of the most common errors writers make in web copy:

- **Mixing up words.** For example, using your (your dog) instead of *you're* (short for you are); *there* (he lives there) instead of *their* (their house); or *accept* (agree to) instead of *except* (excluding).

- **Assuming spellcheck catches everything.** Read your words carefully to make sure they make sense. For example, spell check won't catch *form* if you meant *from*.

- **Using run-on sentences.** These are two or more complete sentences that go on with no punctuation or are joined by commas rather than a semicolon.

- **Using adjectives in place of adverbs.** Adjectives modify a person, place, or thing, while adverbs clarify verbs. An example of a misused adjective:"I ran *good* in the race" instead of "I ran *well* in the race."

- **Using an apostrophe to form the plural of an abbreviation or number.** It's *CDs*, not *CD's*.

Value Sincerity Over Hype

Want to know a great trick for making your prospects and customers think you really care about them? Really care about them. Sure, you can get away with conning your prospects and customers into thinking you're sincere for a while, but the longer the relationship continues, the more likely your true what's-in-it-for-me motives will become apparent. And regardless of what has happened in the past, you'll be lumped back into their just-another-huckster group and they'll take their business elsewhere, as they should.

Rule 3: Use Language that Is Powerful and Meaningful

In order to connect with your readers, you must establish yourself as a trusted resource, industry expert, and take-charge person or company. Therefore, your sales letter copy should convey your confidence, credibility, and professionalism—without being over the top. Here are some tips to help you accomplish these goals:

- Write in an active rather than passive voice. For example, say "The committee approved the policy," not "The policy was approved by the committee."

- Use potent words and phrases such as: *free, easy, enjoy, it's here, just arrived, risk-free, yes,* and *simple.*

- Make your copy flow from one topic to the next by using transitional phrases, such as *here's why, best of all, the truth is, in short, if that's not enough,* and *what's more.*

- Employ action words and phrases such as: *announcing, compare, introducing, sign up today,* and *discover*

Rule 4: Lose the Hard-Sell Language

Numerous research studies confirm that, in general, people do not want to be *sold*, yet they like to *buy*. Not surprisingly, it turns out that the best way to sell (online or otherwise) is to treat your prospects exactly the way you like to be treated when the tables are turned. So, focus on their needs, not sales, and the sales will come.

Thus, consider ways to attract them instead of clobbering them over the head with a hard-sell approach—and that means being careful of the words you use and the messages they convey. Most importantly, don't exaggerate, even if this seems counter-intuitive and the opposite of what you have been taught. Instead, use words that your prospects will find comfortable and believable. Avoid using words and phrases such as *wealth, money-*

Custom Fit Your Language

If you're fortunate enough to know your target prospects intimately, express yourself in the manner they find most acceptable. For instance, if you're selling widgets to engineers, choose words that are logical, and be sure to back up all claims with specific data. Conversely, if you offer customized birthday cards, you'll want to use language that conveys warm emotions. However, let's say you sell pet supplies. In this case, you'll have to do both—appeal to the left-brainers who are looking for practical things (food, shampoo, leashes), and the right-brainers who feel that Fluffy would look adorable in a tiara. You get the idea.

Mary Eule Scarborough,
(www.StrategicMarketingAdvisors.com)

making, fortune, millionaire, mail order, incredible, and so forth.

Rule 5: Talk to Your Visitors' Hearts and Minds

Communication works best when it describes logical, sensible product advantages and evokes positive feelings. This is important because

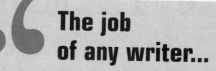

The job of any writer...

is to use ordinary words to convey extraordinary ideas."

—*James Michener, American author*

your target market is usually composed of similar amounts of both; don't make the mistake of appealing only to your prospects' rational or emotional minds (usually referred to as left and right brains). Rather, explain how solving their problems will make them feel and why you offer the best solution.

For instance, if you're selling business-to-business products, stress more practical benefits such as income, efficiency, or speed. However, also describe how your clients will feel when they save time (golf anyone?) and money as a result of using your products. Use your language skills to paint a picture of a beautiful sunny day on the golf course.

Rule 6: Add Some Zing

Even though your copy should be honest and simple it can still be exciting! Turn on your imagination and spice it up with:

- **Controversy.** People love hullabaloo and learn from debate, so don't avoid it! Make a bold statement, then encourage your readers to comment (this works especially well in blogs).

- **Anecdotes.** People love stories, so don't be afraid to tell one.

- **Colorful figures of speech.** Jazz up your copy by using metaphors (comparisons without using *as* or *like*), analogies (parallel stories to show comparisons), and other vivid figures of speech.

- **Power words or phrases.** Use *risk-free, proof, exclusive,* etc. Avoid using meaningless, overused and trite language such as: *quality, the best, #1, we treat customers right,* or *friendly service.*

MUST-HAVE SALES LETTER ELEMENTS

As any good writer knows, written communication can be broken down into standardized elements; when used correctly, these elements result in an effective piece. That's why I've included the following list of essential sales letter elements that you can use as a checklist for developing your own.

A POWERFUL HEADLINE
Do you Know the Single Biggest Mistake Writers Make?

Gotcha! If you're reading this it may be because the headline for this section did exactly what it was supposed to do—grab your attention and stimulate your desire to read more. Your headline, or opening *ta-da*, is the single most important copy component, so craft it very carefully. In order to ensure that you grab your prospects' attention, your headline must be compelling, speak directly to your readers' most pressing problems, and contain your product's most powerful benefit and differentiator.

> ## "On the web it's especially important...
> people are literally whizzing by at the speed of light; clicking everywhere, going from one web site to the next. Your headline has to reach out and grab them."
> —*Yanik Silver, author and publisher*

Although print headlines (e.g., in newspaper columns, magazine articles, and reports) should also compel the audience to read on, your sales letter's headline must go one step further and create an interest in, and desire for, your product or service. So in addition to setting the tone for the rest of your letter, your headline should grab your prospects' *attention*, stimulate their *interest*, increase their *desire* to learn more, and motivate *action*.

Therefore, you should consider getting more aggressive in your letter writing by asking yourself what would get your attention if you were one of your prospects. What headline would make you stop scanning the page and read more (your first goal)?

My view? Try to write something slightly outrageous, yet believable, that can be read in five seconds or less. Following are some tips for creating your own:

- **Use the word *you*.** Remember, your prospects don't care how long you've been in business or how smart you are; they want to know how your products and services will benefit them. (Yes, I'm going to keep repeating this.)

- **Make your headline short or long**. Either length performs well as long as it's no longer than necessary to perform its primary function.

> ## "Advertising experts estimate that...
>
> between 75 percent and 90 percent of any advertising's effectiveness comes from the headline. With a good headline, you stand a fighting chance of having anything from minimal to overwhelming success. But without a good headline, your chances of success are next to zero."
>
> —*David Garfinkel, master copywriter*
> *(www.killercopytactics.com)*

- **Be positive.** For the most part, negativity doesn't work unless it helps you to more accurately pinpoint your readers' problem and offer your solution for eliminating or avoiding it.

- **Use basic design guidelines** (covered in Chapter 4). Position your headline where it is most visible. The eye is naturally drawn to between $2/3$ and $3/4$ of an inch up the page or space. It also helps to position a headline under a photo or graphic, if possible. Set in serif typeface using upper and lower cases (sans serif is best for copy).

- **Be personal.** Let your prospects know you're talking directly to them by using familiar jargon, referring to their city and/or state, and so forth. For instance, if your targeted prospects are stay-at-home moms, use that phrase in your headline.

- **Be specific and believable.** As I said earlier in the chapter, don't exaggerate. Also, it's extremely important to give readers specifics in the headline because it increases believability—and response. Use real numbers, money figures, and dates.

- **Go easy on indirect references, comedy, and abstractions.** They're often confusing and usually get you nowhere.

> ## " A headline that offers topical news...
>
> is often very successful. If your product or service is newsworthy, put that special news announcement right at the top of your ad. If you are promoting a product to one particular group, include a 'red flag' in your headline that will single out these prospects. The key point is: The simple failure to test headlines against each other could cost you more than half of your profit potential."
>
> *—Jay Abraham, marketing expert and author*
> *(www.abraham.com)*

Remember also that you must test, test, test. Never, ever create just one headline! One small word can make a huge difference in your results. If you use subheads (these are optional and mainly used just to provide essential detail missing from the headline) the same general rules apply.

If you are looking for an excellent headline-generator program, I highly recommend an affordable piece of software called Headline Wizard; you can find it at www.Headline Wizard.com.

THEIR PROBLEM AND YOUR SOLUTION

Ask yourself: What is my targeted prospects' biggest problem, and what is my solution for solving it? Remember, they want to believe, really believe, that you can help them, so do just that. Perhaps the biggest barrier to overcome is that many people believe that their problem is unique—let them know it is not. Therefore, you must

- understand your target audience's major problem(s)
- offer proof that the problem is so important that it must be solved immediately
- provide a cure using your products and/or services
- explain why you're the best person or company to resolve it.

BULLET POINTS WITH HOT BENEFITS

Remember that your prospects are focusing on one thing only—themselves. Continually remind yourself that as they read or listen to your message they are asking themselves, "What's in this for me?" Answer this question, and you'll be well on your way.

Now it's time to take the key benefits that you developed for your product or service in Chapter 2 and convert them to bullet points.

TESTIMONIALS THAT SHOW RESULTS

The second most important addition to your sales page is customer testimonials. Since your online prospect can't walk into your store, be greeted with a big smile in person, or watch other happy customers waiting in line to purchase your merchandise, testimonials help reassure visitors that you're the real deal. You'll especially want blurbs from people who express specific and concrete results they experienced due to your product or services (made money, lost weight, and so on).

Because your company's cornerstone philosophy is one of service to others (I hope!) you do good things. Your customers are the smartest and most fortunate consumers on earth. Why? Because you consistently provide them with solutions to their problems. Each time your customers meet with you, or your employees, they congratulate themselves; they know that choosing your company over all others is a wise decision. So why not take advantage of this goodwill and allow them to help you, and others, by expressing their gratitude in the form of a testimonial?

Security in Testimonials

While it's important to establish credibility by providing information about your customers, you must be careful. I recommend an identifier like S. Smith, Dallas, Texas. If your customer's last name is unusual (that is, easy for a stranger to find) try Sally S., Dallas, Texas.

Ideally testimonials are signed with someone's full name and another identifier, such as their city and state or position and company. It's even better if testimonials are from figures well known in your industry.

How do you go about this? The simple answer: ask, especially right after (no longer than a month) their first purchase. Honest testimonials are free and very effective and should be peppered throughout your sales page. Figures 5-1 and 5-2 contain some well-worded testimonials that you can use as guides for generating your own. Note the exact figures documented in these examples.

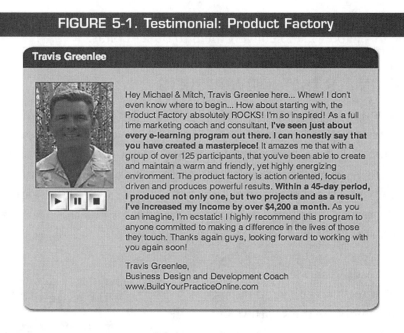

FIGURE 5-1. Testimonial: Product Factory

Travis Greenlee

Hey Michael & Mitch, Travis Greenlee here... Whew! I don't even know where to begin... How about starting with, the Product Factory absolutely ROCKS! I'm so inspired! As a full time marketing coach and consultant, **I've seen just about every e-learning program out there. I can honestly say that you have created a masterpiece!** It amazes me that with a group of over 125 participants, that you've been able to create and maintain a warm and friendly, yet highly energizing environment. The product factory is action oriented, focus driven and produces powerful results. **Within a 45-day period, I produced not only one, but two projects and as a result, I've increased my income by over $4,200 a month.** As you can imagine, I'm ecstatic! I highly recommend this program to anyone committed to making a difference in the lives of those they touch. Thanks again guys, looking forward to working with you again soon!

Travis Greenlee,
Business Design and Development Coach
www.BuildYourPracticeOnline.com

www.90dayproduct.com

Figure 5-2 is a testimonial that Mary Scarborough received regarding her new book, *The Procrastinator's Guide to Marketing: A Pain-Free Solution that Delivers a Profit-Producing Marketing Plan,* which she co-authored with her husband, David A. Scarborough.

Here are some quick tips for getting your testimonials right:

■ **Get them in writing.** Errors are not good when you're quoting someone.

■ **Make sure they support your offer.** This reinforcement helps generate action.

■ **Let your customers know (again, in writing) exactly how theirs will, or may, be used.** Also have them sign a release agreement.

■ **Ask customers to be as specific as possible.** This is far more effective than vague generalizations.

■ **Be sensitive to your customers' concerns about privacy and safety.** Never include their full name and complete address!

FIGURE 5.2 Testimonial: Procrastinator's Guide

I've just finished reading *The Procrastinator's Guide to Marketing* from StrategicMarketingAdvisors.com. What a joy! An excellent new book written in true, easy- to-read style by authors and site founders Mary and David Scarborough.

I've not yet seen anything quite like *The Procrastinator's Guide to Marketing*; it is truly unique! Here's why.

After reviewing this practical, "how to..." gem, I'm reminded of the wonderful quote from Bill Bradley: "Ambition is the path to success. Persistence is the vehicle you arrive in." With that in mind, I would add *"The Procrastinator's Guide to Marketing* is how you can get there." It's really, really good—and I don't say that lightly!

So what's all the fuss about? Simple: when you do what I do, you'll come across lots of smoke and mirrors and bucket loads of pure nonsense that can make your head spin. And that, dear reader, is why I'm genuinely thrilled when I find the opposite: a true marketing guide based on hard won, practical experience combined with smart marketing techniques that work today.

We all do it, don't we: delay, put things off because "I'm too busy right now ..." and so on. That's why I really like *The Procrastinator's Guide to Marketing*. When I'm going off course, it gently pulls me back on route, so that I can get done sooner, better, and spend more time and focus on my core activities.

As you read this book and start using the templates, you almost feel like you have these two expert, approachable authors standing over your shoulder, advising, helping, encouraging, giving you a little push when you need it, so you need never feel stuck at any time.

Templates are a great idea. We use templates to save time and make a task easier. So you won't be disappointed when in addition to the printed book, you can download all the relevant templates, worksheets, samples, resource guides, and examples the authors have formatted especially for the book, free of charge at www.StrategicMarketingAdvisors.com.

What a gift! Amazingly, there must be $100+ value in those time-saving templates alone.

So there you have it. It gets my highest recommendation. Don't waste another second floundering around in confusion: choose clarity and invest in *The Procrastinator's Guide to Marketing* right now while the templates are still included free, and set yourself back on the path to power, success, and achievement.

Even better: buy two copies at the same time: *The Procrastinator's Guide to Marketing* makes an ideal enduring gift for a friend, relative, or colleague.

Brian Austin
www.internettips.com   "smart web promotion—the write way!"

Web designer, technical writer, e-publisher; author of 15 books published in the UK and USA (since 1990); member of the Society of Authors (SoA)

Unique web publishing solutions for non-technical uses: smart, easy, powerful; search engine friendly; stunning, world-class designs

THE POWER POSTSCRIPT

A postscript, or PS, is the second most important element (the first is your headline) to include in all direct-response advertising. Many people read the headline first, then go directly to the PS. This is your opportunity to reinforce and reiterate your most powerful benefit—the one you included in your headline. Obviously, postscripts are most effectively used in sales letters; however, you can still use this technique elsewhere and adapt it as appropriate. In the example in Figure 5-3 from Yanik Silver's Instant Sales Letters web site, the PS is linked to a separate web page that answers the most frequently asked questions.

FIGURE 5-3. Postscript

P.S. Click here if you've decided not to order.

P.P.S. Just think! You'll never again suffer through the pain and hassle of trying to write a powerful sales letter yourself. Or pay big bucks hiring a top copywriter. Now, you can get everything all done for you, practically handed to you on a silver platter. You simply fill-in-the-blanks...and you're done in about 2 ½ minutes -- flat!

(Order now through our Secure Server, and get instant access!)
Click Here Now

CALL TO ACTION

Another curious thing about human nature is that we often want what we can't have. So how can you use this trait effectively? First create an offer that has time limits built in and compels your readers to act or make a choice sooner than later. Then steer them to the right choice.

An easy way to understand the call to action concept is to put yourself in your prospects' place and draw from your own experiences as a consumer (what valuable resources!). Express a sense of urgency so your prospects understand that it is in their best interest to perform the desired action right away. Why? Because if they don't act immediately, they are far less likely to act at all. This bears repeating: When interested prospects don't act immediately, there is a good chance that they never will.

Another good tip is to always provide a reason for acting. Invite your prospects to do business with you, then make it easy for them to say yes! Consider tactics such as free pickup and delivery; additional savings, products, or services for immediate response; and time-sensitive offers. For example, do the opposite of what most people do when selling online. Instead of saying, "Here you are, come and buy it," say something like, "I've got only 1,000 copies of my e-book available until December 25th. After that, I'm not selling any more." Then sometime after December 25th, announce your reasons for not selling any more.

Does this mean you're out of business? No. The reason you're not selling your e-book after December 25th may be that you're revising it, and the updated version will be ready for sale on January 10th. You get the idea. The bottom line is that you want your prospects to recognize that they really might miss out on something special if they don't act now.

WHY IT WOULD BE FOOLISH TO DO BUSINESS WITH ANYONE OTHER THAN YOU

After you've aptly described your prospects' problem(s), let them know how you, your products, and/or your services provide the solutions they want. But that's not good enough; you must also tell them *why*. In other words, explain why you offer the *very best* solution. For example, tell them why you're the best person to handle their investments; why you're positive they're going to love their new hairstyle; or why your seafood is the freshest in town. Essentially, explain why folks should patronize you instead of your competitors.

After this, the rubber meets the road. If any of your claims are untrue, unrealistic, or undeliverable, do not use them! Don't make promises you can't keep. Period. And never compete solely on price. It will get you nowhere fast.

Compete on the value you deliver even if your inexpensive pricing is a major benefit to your prospects. In this case, explain why you're able to offer such exceptionally superior products or services at such reasonable rates.

UNCONDITIONAL GUARANTEE

The idea of a money-back refund or product guarantee is not a new one. Who hasn't heard "If you're not satisfied with our product, simply return it within 30 days and we'll refund your money"? Or how about "Try it for a week. If you're not happy, return it and we'll refund the full purchase amount, less shipping." These are your average, run-of-the-mill, boilerplated guarantees.

At first sight they sound reasonable, but I think they are equally flawed. Why? First, they admit that the customer may be dissatisfied or unhappy. If you're delivering the promised experience, this can't happen! Second, they place a time limit on satisfaction. If you're confident, this is never necessary. Finally, they both guarantee to refund the initial investment (and one even keeps the shipping costs), but neither does anything to pay back the customer for his aggravation and disappointment!

You must make your guarantee more effective, because it is an essential ingredient in all marketing communication. The governing rule is simple: Your guarantee is your promise. It is meant to remove, not merely reduce, the buyer's risk. Here are some tips for getting it right:

- Reconsider time-sensitive refunds. Extend yours longer than anyone else in your industry or, if possible, for the lifetime of the product.

- Let prospects try before they buy—no strings attached.

- Provide free samples of your product or service.

- Offer a no-questions-asked full refund plus a suitable amount (about $5) just for trying.

That said, there are some exceptions you may consider. For example, if you run a 12-week course, you may not want to offer an unlimited guarantee, because it may encourage some people to drop out or request a refund if they decide not to do the required work. In cases like this, you might offer them freeenrollment in your next class or a partial refund. Ultimately the decision is up to you.

PRICING INFORMATION AND PAYMENT OPTIONS

You must be easy to do business with, and part of being easy is allowing your customers to pay you with whatever form of currency they find most acceptable. At a minimum you should accept all major credit cards, personal and traveler's checks, debit cards, money orders, and electronic checks (if possible).

Also, since you're conducting business over the internet it is important to allow customers to pay securely through their PayPal account or with other online services. It also helps to offer customers the choice of paying by check over the phone, and many consumers (and companies) are discovering the benefits of setting up authorized automatic monthly payment accounts.

TEST, TEST, TEST

After you've composed an exceptional sales letter (with the tips in this chapter) it's time to run it. Then change it. For example, create two identical sales pages and change only one element, paragraph, headline, or offer at a time. Then test the results and retire the underperformer (the one that gets lower results) to your archives.

Repeat the process and test the new version against your last winner. Again, retire the loser. Do this one more time with yet another page. Retire the loser. Go with the one that wins, at least for the time being. When funds allow, repeat this three-round test with new sales letters.

WEB WORK: YOUR INTERACTIVE ADVENTURE

1. REACHING YOUR PROSPECTS

To make sure your web copy gets on the right track, answer these questions:

■ What are your prospects' greatest problems? Be specific.

■ What are your solutions to these problems? Be specific.

■ Write three attention-grabbing headlines for your web page. (If this is difficult consider purchasing the headline generating software at www. HeadlineWizard.com.)

2. USING COPY ELEMENTS

Go to your favorite e-commerce web sites—particularly ones where you've purchased products and/or services. Then make a list of the copy elements that increased your interest. See which elements you can add to your site.

3. WRITING WITH STYLE

Review the copywriting style points discussed in this chapter and modify your existing sales letter with them in mind.

CHAPTER 5 REMINDERS

Before moving on to Chapter 6, "Traffic Conversion: The Key to Increased Sales and List Building," let's take a minute to review the most important lessons learned from this chapter:

■ Your sales letter headline and primary bullet points should contain your most important product or service benefits.

■ Don't lose credibility with poorly written copy.

■ Include a strong and clear call-to-action in all of your sales copy.

■ A postscript (or PS) is the second most important element in your sales letter.

> ## Regardless of what you write,
> your words should improve the blank space they replaced."
>
> —*Mary Eule Scarborough, speaker, marketing export, and author*

TRAFFIC CONVERSION

The Key to Increased Sales and List Building

In this chapter you'll learn

- *the goal of web traffic conversion*

- *the biggest mistake online marketers make and how to avoid it*

- *why conversion is a lot like dating*

- *the essentials for improving conversion rates*

...and much more.

" **Converting a web visitor to a paying customer...**

is a lot like dating. No one in their right mind would propose marriage on a first date, yet that is exactly what most web sites do by asking for the sale before first developing a relationship."

—*Mitch Meyerson, author and speaker*

Throughout my career, I have consulted with hundreds of clients who asked for my guidance in developing their e-commerce web sites. And in just about every instance, they indicated their first and primary goal was traffic; they wanted people to find and visit their web site. They firmly, but erroneously, believed that their online success depended only on the number of visitors they were able to attract. They mistakenly equated traffic with sales. So they over-focused on bringing hoards of people to their site, without doing the work necessary to ensure that once their visitors arrived, they'd act.

The result? Their traffic increased, but they ended up

- wasting valuable effort and money, because their visitors did not turn into leads, sales, or repeat customers
- squandering their precious time, by reinventing the wheel unnecessarily rather than using proven strategies from the online marketing superstars
- disappointing interested visitors and prospects, who left their site and didn't return.

That's why I've chosen to discuss visitor conversion before traffic. This may seem counterintuitive, but think about your web site as a storefront downtown. Would you hold an open house without first deciding on special sales promotions, lining up entertainment, creating visual appeal, or ordering refreshments? While you'll certainly invite people to your web site, don't do so until it's ready. To do otherwise will lead to failure.

In this chapter I teach you ways to optimize your web site—that is, get your physical environment ready—so your prospects and customers will be compelled to opt in to your mailing list; learn more about your products and/or services; and feel comfortable purchasing from you. Once you understand and apply these conversion tactics, you'll

- geometrically increase your qualified leads and customers
- construct small web site changes that make big differences
- boost your conversion rates and visitor value.

In order to do this, you'll first need to learn the basics, which will serve as the philosophical foundation for creating your conversion strategies.

WHAT IS THE GOAL OF CONVERSION?

Traffic conversion is a committed process for building relationships and rapport with your targeted audience; it helps visitors to know, like, and trust you. When done correctly, it provides the opportunity for online marketers to achieve their ultimate objective of acquiring and retaining loyal and profitable customers. For some, the conversion journey is a straight and speedy highway leading directly to a sale, but the vast majority must be prepared to take a slower, more methodical route.

Traffic conversion begins with a direct response request—an invitation for your guests to complete a desired action. That action must be one that transforms your

- **visitors** (people who may be looking for your products or services and have dropped in to check out your site) **into prospects**

- **prospects** (those who have chosen to take a closer look by opting into your e-mail list) **into customers**

- **customers** (people who purchase your products and/or services, also known as clients, patrons, patients, consumers, buyers) **into raving fans** (life-time customers).

This building process begins with identifying, in advance, the specific and measurable actions you'll request. For example:

- real estate agents who want their prospects to call their office to set up an appointment

- service professionals who ask their visitors to opt in to their mailing list

- healthcare providers who invite their prospects to subscribe to their monthly newsletter

- marketing experts who want their visitors to sign up for their weekend seminar.

In order to achieve this, you'll need to create an online environment that ensures that your audience feels welcomed in a warm and sincere way and makes it easy for them to take action. It's similar to inviting people to your

Why Consumers Make Those Choices

Jay Conrad Levinson, author of *Guerrilla Marketing*, cites a famous study in which more than 10,000 consumers rated the reasons they chose one company over another. Here are the top five factors they chose, in order:

1. Confidence
2. Quality
3. Service
4. Selection
5. Price

home. I'm sure that you greet your guests at the door with a broad smile, a handshake, or hug; offer them something to drink or eat; suggest they sit in the most comfortable chair; and so forth. You don't bombard them with stories about how great you are, request a loan or ask to borrow their car, or leave them on their own to wander aimlessly around your house. This may seem like a far-fetched illustration, but it may be more apt than you think, because it provides the perfect segue (and an opportunity for another relevant analogy) into a conversation on one of the biggest mistakes online marketers make.

EXPECTING A SALE ON THE FIRST VISIT

Remember my dating analogy from Chapter 3—the one where marriage was proposed on the first date? Sounded pretty ridiculous, didn't it? But as I said then, it's not all that dissimilar from asking your online visitors to buy on their first visit.

Healthy relations of all kinds are built gradually and it's no different in the online world. It's important to get to know your visitors, build trust, and allow them to warm up to you before asking for a sale. However, most e-commerce entrepreneurs do just the opposite and insist upon pressuring their prospects into buying instantly.

HOW DO YOU BUILD SUSTAINABLE RELATIONSHIPS?

The simple answer is one step at a time. This process begins with the understanding that you must do everything in your power to make your visitor feel comfortable and confident that your offer is the best solution to their problem (the number one reason that people choose to do business with one company over others).

Let's go back to our dating couple. Here is a more logical scenario for a relationship that builds up to a marriage proposal: A man and woman have a chance encounter at party. They notice one another and instantly decide that they're interested. The man walks over to the woman and begins a casual conversation about the weather, sports, careers, or mutual friends. Before leaving he asks her out. She agrees.

- **Date 1:** The couple go out to dinner and start to get to know each other. They ask each other questions, share some of their past experiences, and perhaps talk more about their interests and passions.
- **Date 2:** Our couple enjoys a picnic at the park, a hiking trek on a scenic nature trail, or a long lunch at a small French café.
- **Dates 3 and 4:** They go to the movies and dinner on Saturday night and to a college football game with a group of his friends on Sunday.
- **Date 5:** They spend a long, relaxing weekend together at a quaint bed-and-breakfast.
- **Date 6:** They go out to dinner with her parents, who are visiting from out of town. The next day, he plays golf with her father.
- **Dates 7, 8, 9, and 10:** She's at his place or he's at her place four evenings a week.
- **Dates 11 through 60:** Same as above, only it's six days per week.
- **After the 60th date,** they're no longer dating; they're living together and discussing their future together. They get married a year after that.

Although a marriage proposal and a sale are different in many ways, they are quite similar in that they each require time and commitment. Great relationships—either personal or professional—don't happen overnight. So let's see how our dating sequence might translate to building relationships with prospects via your e-commerce site. (Specifics will vary for your industry.)

- **Visit 1:** Complete strangers—your targeted prospects—visit your web site. They look it over and instantly decide if they like what they see. If not,

> ## "All things come to him who waits...
>
> provided he knows what he is waiting for."
>
> —*Woodrow T. Wilson, U.S. President*

they leave. If so, they hang around a bit longer to check it out further.

If they think your web site looks professional, your copy is compelling and well written, and your product and/or service solutions are relevant, they'll be pleased to learn that you're offering a free teleconference where you'll provide them with actionable tips for solving their problem. Understanding that you've just given them a risk-free method for trying before buying and eager to learn more, they provide their name and e-mail address (opt in) in exchange for a reserved spot on the call. Now these strangers are interested prospects.

■ **Visit 2:** After you demonstrate that you deliver on your promises by broadcasting a stimulating, thought-provoking, and content-rich mini course or excellent special report, your prospects are jazzed and can't wait to learn more. Their online visit is longer this time. They ask more questions and dig a little deeper. However, they still may be hesitant to plunk down their hard-earned money and decide instead to take you up on your offer for a one-time, $10, 30-minute telephone counseling session. With little to lose, they gladly pay the small fee and schedule the call.

■ **Visit 3:** Now they're really impressed and see you as an expert in the industry—one who can help them. You were attentive, informative, and pleasant during the call. Once again, you demonstrated that you could be trusted by answering their questions professionally and honestly. And even though you were careful to focus most of the call on their specific challenges, you did invite them to purchase your affordable e-book for further guidance.

■ **Visit 4:** They buy your $19.95 e-book or comparable item.

■ **Visit 5, 6, 7:** They loved the advice and insights you shared in the e-book and know they'll get even more out of your four-week course. They think about it and perhaps visit a time or two more, but eventually, they enroll in your $599 seminar.

BUILDING RELATIONSHIPS TAKES TIME AND REQUIRES PATIENCE

Be prepared to devote the time and patience necessary to turn prospects into customers—it doesn't happen overnight! Consider this:

- 37 percent of interested prospects take 0–3 months to become customers
- 28 percent of interested prospects take 3–6 months to become customers
- 18 percent of interested prospects take 6–12 months to become customers
- 17 percent of interested prospects take more than one year to become customers

And did you know that

- 48 percent of salespeople give up after the first contact
- 25 percent more give up after the second contact
- 12 percent stop trying after the third contact
- 5 percent cease after the fourth contact
- 90 percent of leads never get followed up more than four times

Make Mine Automated, Please

If you're too busy to follow up, you can automate the entire process using sequential auto responders, which deliver handcrafted e-mail messages at the intervals you choose. For an example, visit www.EasyWebAutomation.com.

The moral of the story? You must be committed to devoting the time and patience necessary to the conversion process. Don't give up!

Now let's take a look at what every web site needs to achieve outstanding conversion rates.

GENERAL WEB SITE CONVERSION ESSENTIALS

Converting visitors to repeat customers takes a lot more than simply offering a good product at a great price or filling your page with celebrity testimonials. Today you need more… much more. That's why it's important to understand the two types of conversion strategies—opt-in and sales conversions—how they differ, and ways to make them work for you. But before I go into more detail on each, let me first provide you with the following three most essential web site elements for improving any type of conversion.

1. Make it professional looking, eye-catching, and well written.

- Spend a few extra dollars on a quality web and/or graphic designer. Your conversion rates will increase dramatically if your site is well designed. Visitors will view you as the real deal—someone who is confident, competent, experienced, capable, and authentic.

- Add real company elements, such as telephone numbers, physical address, photographs, your logo, the ability to view or pay bills online (if applicable), logos of respected consumer groups or companies like PayPal, ScanAlert, VeriSign, and so on.

- Make sure your sales letter copy is compelling, well written, and error free.

2. Make it uncomplicated and easy to use.

- Make sure your navigation is simple and your visitors understand exactly what to do, by using elements such as a strong call to action, direct links to other pages or information, easily located opt-in boxes, and sales buttons.

- Use the minimum number of pages necessary to provide the information your visitors want to know—nothing more. Don't add layers to your site just because you can.

3. Make it warm and welcoming.

- Remember, your web site is like your home. Welcome your guests with open arms and offer to lighten their load by giving them something of value.

- Don't forget that how you say things is as important as what you say.

OPT-IN CONVERSIONS

The first type of conversion is permission-based marketing tactics, more commonly referred to as *opt-ins*. Simply said, it means that your visitors voluntarily provide their names and e-mail addresses, granting you permission to e-mail them marketing communication. Please pay particular attention to this important distinction! You can't send e-mails to people unless they've given you this information—if you do, it's called spamming, and it's against the law.

In theory, opt-in conversions work very simply. You give your prospects something valuable for free—information, software, a CD, a newsletter subscription—in exchange for their name and e-mail address.

Tactics for Increasing Your Opt-In List

Following are some specific tactics for improving your opt-in conversions, since your database of prospects and customers will be your e-commerce site's most valuable asset.

As you read through these suggestions, keep in mind that the size of your list is not nearly as important as the quality. You are better off having fewer qualified and interested prospects (your target market) than tons of warm

The Lowdown on Spam

Although spamming usually involves abusing the internet's electronic messaging system by sending unsolicited bulk messages, it can also be applied to similar misuse in other media such as Usenet newsgroups, search engines, blogs, and mobile phone and fax transmissions. On December 16, 2003, President George Bush signed the CAN-SPAM Act. This law outlines specific standards for commercial e-mail and requires the Federal Trade Commission to enforce its provisions.

Although there is still some debate about the origin of the term *spam*, many believe it was first coined by the comedy group Monty Python, who sang, "Spam, spam, spam, spam, spam, spam, spam, spam, lovely spam, wonderful spam…" and compared it to an endless repetition of worthless words. Others give credit to a group of southern California computer lab students who noted that the practice reminded them of the lunchmeat Spam in these ways:

- No one wants it, let alone asks for it.
- Although it's actually tasty sometimes, it's the first thing to get pushed aside when there's something better to eat.
- 1 percent of people really love it.

bodies. It's not about getting everyone on the bus; it's about getting the right people on the bus. For example, if you're selling e-books on boats, having a list filled with people who live in the middle of a desert won't do you much good.

Here are some specific visual tactics you can use for improving your conversion rates:

■ **Location, Location, Location.** Make sure your opt-in box is positioned "above the fold"—the section of your web page that can be read without scrolling up or down. Many experts agree that most online visitors look at the right-hand side of a web page first, so you should consider using this area for your opt-in box (see Figure 6-1).

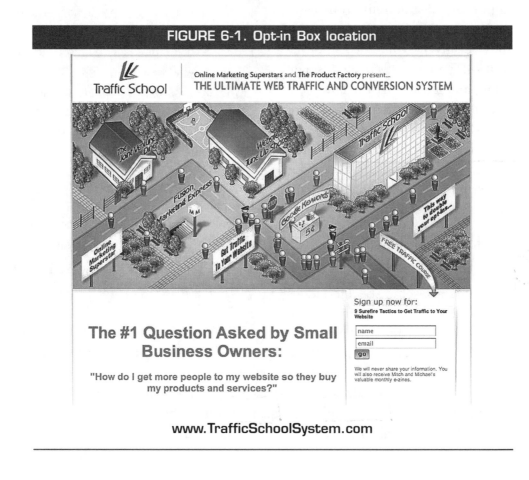

FIGURE 6-1. Opt-in Box location

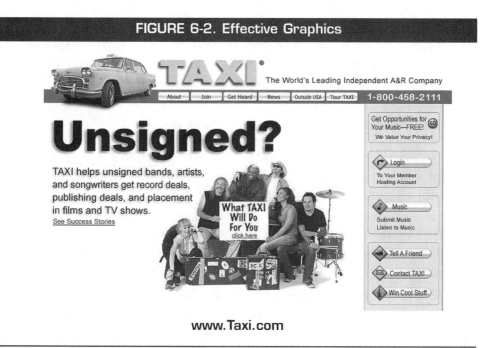

FIGURE 6-2. Effective Graphics

www.Taxi.com

- **Attention-Grabbing Graphics.** Although you shouldn't confuse your visitors with too many pictures or artwork, feel free to go bold on graphics (e.g., stronger colors, more daring designs, arrows, etc.). This will direct your readers' eyes to the most important information. For example, www.Taxi.com uses engaging graphics combined with simple navigation and a powerful headline to encourage its target market of unsigned artists to read more (see Figure 6-2).

- **An Irresistible Offer.** Often referred to as an ethical bribe, this is your opportunity to offer valuable freebies, such as newsletters, e-courses, access to a members-only area, surveys, software downloads, white papers, and e-books.

As the number of broadband connections continues to grow, it will be even easier to offer multiple irresistible freebies and bundle them together. If you'd like to see an example of how I use these, check out my site: www.MitchMeyerson.com.

■ **A Privacy Policy Statement.** This is one of the most effective, yet underrated elements for improving conversions. Be sure to let people know you value them as prospects or customers and promise never to share or rent your mailing list without their permission. Additionally your opt-in box should have a direct link to your privacy policy page. Here's an example of a very brief privacy policy:

> We will not rent, trade, or release your information to any third party for any reason—*ever*. We respect your e-mail privacy and hate spam with a passion.

■ **One-Step Sign-Up.** Make it easy for your visitors to sign up. Don't make them click on multiple pages just to give you their name and e-mail address.

■ **A Squeeze Page.** Also referred to as a single opt-in page, it gives your visitors two choices—opt in or leave. Although at first it may seem like a high-pressure sales tactic (and its name doesn't help), it is not. The truth is that many people want to get to the bottom line faster or feel less distracted with an either-or choice. Most importantly, recent consumer research suggests that these types of pages are extremely effective for increasing opt-ins.

And just to demonstrate, once again, that I practice what I preach, check out Figure 6-3, a screen shot from my own squeeze page.

SALES CONVERSIONS

The second type of conversion strategy is an opt-in box that is used exclusively for sales. Simply said, it means that your visitors actually purchase your product or service online using their credit card, PayPal account, and/or bank or electronic check. As the saying goes, this is where the rubber meets the road. Your prospects will either make a purchase or get cold feet and leave. Your job is to ensure that they choose the former. So let's take a closer look at some tactics you can use to improve your sales conversions.

Building a Responsive Online Mailing List

Craig Perrine—speaker, author, and founder of MaverickMarketer.com—has helped thousands build profitable e-mail subscriber lists and generate millions in sales worldwide from lists big and small. Imagine that you have a list of e-mail addresses and that whenever you send out a promotion, the orders flood in like a tidal wave. That's the dream of every internet marketer and the reality for those who know how to build a list of buyers (instead of just a list of subscribers).

Here are Craig's seven tips for building a responsive list that will put you ahead of 99 percent of your competition:

1. Know what your target market wants badly enough to pay money for. This may sound like obvious advice, but too many businesses try to promote what they want to sell instead of what their prospects want to buy. You can't get people to opt in to your list these days unless you truly offer them something they want badly.

2. Offer people a taste of what you have to sell. Whether you sell them something cheap and put them on your list of customers or offer a free sample (report, e-course, trial) doesn't matter. Just make sure that you make it so that the first transaction they have with you is a no-brainer.

3. Put your offer where your subscribers are. You know what they want, now figure out how you can let them know that you've got what they want. Online, consider targeted pay-per-click ads, articles, forums, and blog posts.

4. Sell the opt-in as if it were expensive, even if it's free. No one wants to give you their e-mail address anymore, it seems, unless they really want what you're offering. You can't just slap an opt-in form on your site and expect much these days. You have to treat your opt-in page like a mini-sales letter for joining your list.

5. Make the opt-in process simple. Your form should be clearly seen and the directions should be spelled out. Keep it short and sweet. If your opt-in process is clunky, the traffic coming to your site won't convert well into subscribers.

6. Follow up consistently. Once you have your new subscribers, stay in touch. One of the biggest mistakes marketers make is not mailing often enough.

7. Set expectations up front. If you have a daily tip newsletter, tell your subscriber that's what they'll get. If you only mail out once a week or a month, let them know that, too. Just make sure that you send them what they are expecting to get.

FIGURE 6-3. One-Stop Sign Up

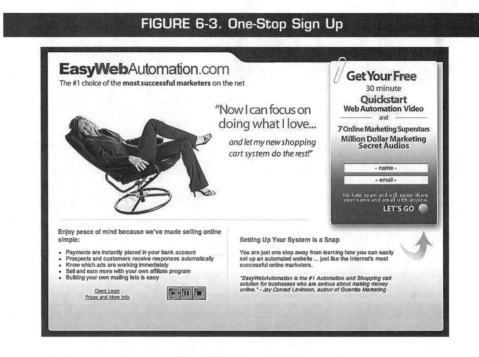

www.EasyWebAutomation.com

Simple Tactics for Improving Sales Conversions

■ **A Dedicated Sales Page.** A sales page is designed to encourage one or more purchases. As discussed in Chapter 5, its objective is to engage the reader emotionally, get them to read more, and take action. See the example in Figure 6-4; to read the full page of this sales copy, go to www.90dayproduct.com.

■ **Obvious "Buy Now" Buttons.** Like your words, your graphics should also contain a strong call to action. This can be achieved using devices such as noticeable purchase buttons (e.g., Buy Now or Order Now) that are placed strategically throughout the site, or a simple line of type to click for results. Figure 6-5 shows how www.HeadlineWizard.com has a clear and obvious place to: "Click Here to Order."

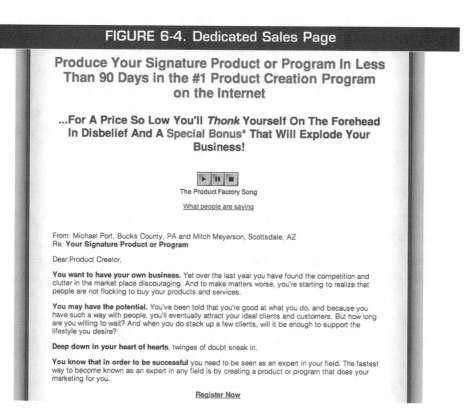

FIGURE 6-4. Dedicated Sales Page

Produce Your Signature Product or Program In Less Than 90 Days in the #1 Product Creation Program on the Internet

...For A Price So Low You'll *Thonk* Yourself On The Forehead In Disbelief And A Special Bonus* That Will Explode Your Business!

The Product Factory Song

What people are saying

From: Michael Port, Bucks County, PA and Mitch Meyerson, Scottsdale, AZ
Re: **Your Signature Product or Program**

Dear Product Creator,

You want to have your own business. Yet over the last year you have found the competition and clutter in the market place discouraging. And to make matters worse, you're starting to realize that people are not flocking to buy your products and services.

You may have the potential. You've been told that you're good at what you do, and because you have such a way with people, you'll eventually attract your ideal clients and customers. But how long are you willing to wait? And when you do stack up a few clients, will it be enough to support the lifestyle you desire?

Deep down in your heart of hearts, twinges of doubt sneak in.

You know that in order to be successful you need to be seen as an expert in your field. The fastest way to become known as an expert in any field is by creating a product or program that does your marketing for you.

Register Now

www.90DayProduct.com

FIGURE 6-5. Purchase Button

You Are Losing Sales Every Minute You Don't Have This Product

"Powerful New Software Automatically Creates Profit-Pulling Headlines In 17 Seconds Flat... And It's Push-Button Easy!"

Click Here To Order Headline Wizard
(Only $47.00 for a lifetime of incredible headlines)

www.HeadlineWizard.com

- **A Reassuring Checkout Page.** Industry experts estimate that a large number of online shoppers abandon a shopping cart before their purchase is completed. To avoid this situation, make sure your order page looks and feels like your other pages; is branded with your logo and other identifying elements; reassures prospects that they've made a wise selection; contains a recap of their purchased items with all pricing information; and clearly states what they should do next.

More Advanced Tactics for Improving Sales Conversions

Here are some more sophisticated conversion tactics for those who want to give them a try:

- **Involvement Devices.** I can't think of better examples of effective involvement devices—tools that help build rapport by enabling your visitors to become more engaged, such as assessment forms, ask campaigns, check boxes, quizzes, and surveys—than those used by online marketing superstar Maria Veloso. Notice in Figure 6-6 how she adds check boxes to get the reader to become more involved.

- **Consumption Strategies.** It's wonderful when you've made a sale, but it isn't enough. For example, just because your customers download your e-book, it doesn't mean they're going to read it. And if they don't consume or use the product or service they purchased, how can they spread positive word-of-mouth referrals?

  That's why it's a good idea to remind new customers to do just that. This can be accomplished easily using web-based automation software. I'll discuss this tactic in great detail in the next chapter.

- **Bundles, Add-ons, Up-Sells, and Bounce-backs.** You may be familiar with McDonald's bundles, add-ons, and up-sells, which go something like this: "Would like fries with your meal?" or "If you order number four, you'll only pay an extra 40 cents and get an order of fries and large drink," or "Why buy one double cheeseburger when you can get three for 50 cents more?"

  These tactics have earned the company millions of dollars because they all result in a higher transactional dollar amount (i.e., more money) and

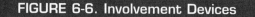

FIGURE 6-6. Involvement Devices

Here's a quick marketing **quiz** that could make a *dramatic impact* on the amount of **money** you earn on the Web. Answer these 5 questions:

(Simply check YES or NO)

1. Do you want to learn **psychological devices** you can use on your website that can make people pull out their credit cards and buy what you're selling? YES ▨ NO ▨

2. Do you want a **website that sells phenomenally well** even during the worst economic times -- even in highly competitive markets -- and even when the price of your product or service is well above your competitors' prices? YES ▨ NO ▨

3. Do you want to **boost your website sales and profits** <u>significantly</u> *without spending a single penny*? YES ▨ NO ▨

www.WebCopywritingUniversity.com

they work well because their consumers have already made a decision to purchase, and feel better because they're getting a bigger bang for their buck. Even better, the bundled products make sense together— that is, they're a logical extension of each other!

It's relatively easy to use this exact same strategy on your e-commerce site. Simply look for commonsense products or services that you can add, bundle, or use to improve your core offering and invite customers to take advantage of them on your order page. For example, let's assume you're selling an e-book on ways to market e-commerce businesses. Your customers might be willing to purchase the e-book and a program that automatically creates headlines (such as the one found on www. HeadlineWizard.com)—especially if they are bundled together and discounted. And there's no better time or place to offer packaged deals than on your checkout page. One of my online marketing superstars claims that this strategy alone resulted in a 37 percent increase in sales.

Another advanced tactic you can use at the time of sale is a bounce-back offer. This is an offer that gets your customer to return and order from you again. Bounce-back specialist Blaine Oelkers puts it this way: "One of your most effective 'moments of power' in your business is at the time of sale." He says that it's at that precise moment that you want to:

1. thank your customers for ordering

2. let them know they made a great decision to buy from you

3. give them an aggressive offer to bounce back and purchase again from you right away.

Consider offering a cash discount for the next order, a percent off, free shipping, or even a free gift with their next purchase. For more examples of profitable bounce-back offers, visit www.BouncebackProfits.com.

■ **Exit Strategies.** When people decide to leave your site you may still have one more chance to make a sale by using a pop-up generator program (they come with some shopping carts). An exit message is contained in a small pop-up box that opens right as people click to leave your web site. For more details on exit strategies read Chapter 24 of my book *Success Secrets of the Online Marketing Superstars.*

METRICS 101: WHAT YOU NEED TO KNOW

Since you can't improve what you don't measure, you should be asking yourself questions such as:

■ How many visitors come to my web site?

■ How many visitors opt in to my e-mail list?

■ How many people click on the buy buttons?

■ What is my visitor value?

It's vitally important that you find out the answers and analyze the results. Otherwise you won't know what to continue doing and what to stop.

Headlines, bullet points, and other elements are easy to change, and they can affect your results dramatically, so it pays to monitor them closely. Moreover, your strategic partners will use your sales figures to help them decide whether or not they are willing to promote your products and/or services.

Also, in order to know what you can reasonably spend on a pay-per-click campaign (I discuss this in Chapter 9), you need to know how

Partner Up!

What is a JV partner? JV stands for joint venture, which is also known as fusion marketing or a strategic alliance partner. Simply put, this happens when you enter into a win-win business arrangement with others—they promote your products; you promote theirs, and/or you promote each other's.

much one visitor is worth; otherwise, you'll risk losing your shirt! Here's a simple formula for calculating your average visitor value:

Price of the product x Number of sales ÷ Number of visitors = Average visitor value

Here is a straightforward example of how yours might look. Let's assume the following is true:

- You offer only one product for sale.
- Each sells for $97.
- On average, you sell two products for every 100 visitors (2 percent conversion rate)

Based on this, your average visitor value is $1.94. Here's why:

$$(\$97 \times 2) = \$194 \div (100) = \$1.94$$

Clearly, you need to know this before you invest in pay-per-click campaigns, or you could end up spending more per click than you earn!

USING AD TRACKERS TO CALCULATE METRICS

In many shopping cart systems, there is a feature called an ad tracker that determines how many people click on your link and subsequently buy your product. Additionally, it automatically calculates your visitor value. I discuss ad trackers further in Chapter 7.

TEST BEFORE YOU INVEST

As I've said before, you must be prepared to test, test, test. This is even more important when it comes to conversions. That's why it's a good idea to make sure that your ad-tracking feature allows you to conduct split testing. *Split testing* works like this: Every time visitors click a link in an e-mail you have sent them, they will be alternately directed to one of two or three differently designed sales pages. Each page will have a different headline, photo, pricing, graphical layout, or any other features that you want to test. Using your ad-tracking program, you'll quickly be able to determine which web page results in the most conversions—sales and/or opt ins.

> # Test, test, and then test again.
>
> Never stop testing everything. You want to test your advertising, styles, colors, etc. Test your offer, test your price, and test different types of advertising. The key is to test small. If it works, apply it to everything you know."
>
> —*Corey Rudl, founder of the Internet Marketing Center*

Once you have a winner, retire the others and continue to use the winner as the benchmark for testing other elements. But as I said previously, you should change only one element at a time or you'll never be sure what's driving the results!

WEB WORK: YOUR INTERACTIVE ADVENTURE

1. Score your web site on a scale of 1–10 (10 meaning very strong) in the following areas:

    ■ Professional looking, eye-catching, and well-written: _____

    ■ Uncomplicated and easy to use: _____

    ■ Warm and welcoming: _____

2. Evaluate your web site for opt-in conversions and implement at least three to five improvements suggested in this chapter. Then get feedback from others.

3. Evaluate your web site for sales conversions and implement at least three to five improvements suggested in this chapter. Then get feedback from others.

4. Calculate the following metrics:

   ■ The number of people that visit your web site (www.google/analytics is a great free tracking program)

   ■ The number of people who opt in to your mailing list

   ■ The number of people who visit your order page

   ■ The number of people who buy your product

   ■ Your visitor value

CHAPTER 6 REMINDERS

Before moving to Chapter 7, "Automation: The Key to Increasing E-Commerce Profits," let's take a minute to review the most important lessons learned from this chapter:

   ■ Conversion goals are to turn visitors into prospects into customers into raving fans.

   ■ Your web site's look, feel, and ease of navigation are essential to conversion. You have only one chance to make a good first impression.

   ■ Your opt-in box must be prominent and offer something irresistible.

   ■ Your order page must reassure your customers that they are making the right decision.

   ■ You can improve only what you can measure, so learn how to calculate your metrics and always look for ways to test and improve your site.

CHAPTER 7

AUTOMATION

The Key to Increasing E-Commerce Profits

In this chapter you'll learn

- *the benefits of automation*

- *ways to use the power of sequential autoresponders*

- *tips for creating targeted sublists*

- *the ins and outs of merchant accounts and PayPal*

- *all about shopping carts*

...and much more.

" **The strategic use of automation**

defines who wins when applying e-commerce solutions. With the power of automation, you'll see your online sales and profits excel beyond what you ever thought possible."

—*Rob Bell, from* Success Secrets of the Online Marketing Superstars

Do you ever feel like you just can't get it all done? Are you leaving important things, like staying in touch with customers and prospects, unfinished because you're just too overwhelmed with work? Do you worry about your unanswered e-mails or phone messages? Do you plan to write online articles, add fresh content to your web site, and/or begin a blog, but wonder where you'll find the time? Are things just getting away from you?

If so, you're like many other online marketers. Let's face it; time is more valuable than ever before. Given the complexities of owning and managing a business, the increase in worldwide competition, and the onslaught of information we receive, most entrepreneurs spend most of their day just trying to keep their heads above water. As a result, they wear themselves out working, working, working—and getting nowhere fast. The answer to why this happens is simple: They're working on the wrong things! Instead of devoting their limited time to tasks that will help them grow their business—writing compelling sales copy, developing strategic partnerships, participating in online discussions and forums, overseeing pay-per-click campaigns, and the like—they are consumed with their day-to-day administrative and operation duties. Figure 7-1 is a simple illustration of how this looks for many entrepreneurs.

Looks overwhelming, doesn't it? No wonder so many entrepreneurs are stretched to their breaking point! One person—or even two—cannot effectively handle this many tasks by themselves. But fear not; nowadays you don't have to!

In addition to being the most effective time-saving tools available, automation programs are an internet marketer's best friend, hands down. As a matter of fact, when I'm asked to name the number one e-commerce web site marketing tool, I don't even hesitate. These software gems allow you to reap the benefits of work you've already completed, over and over again. And while it will take you some time to set up your system, you'll get that back, 20-fold. Simply said, there are so many benefits to automation programs that if you're serious about growing and sustaining a profitable online business, you'd be foolish to ignore them. Following are just a few of these benefits. You will:

- **Save time.** Once you have programmed and scheduled the automatic communication, you can send messages to prospects and customers no

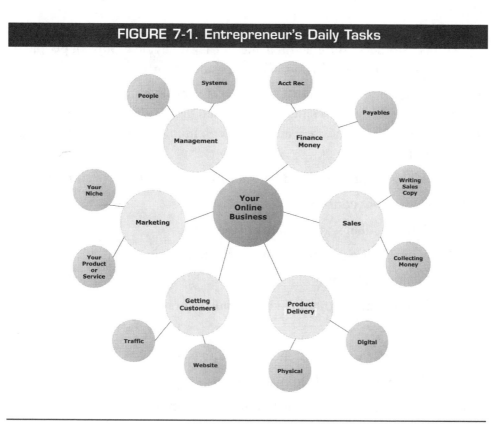

FIGURE 7-1. Entrepreneur's Daily Tasks

matter where you are or what else you're doing. You can maintain positive relationships even when stuff happens.

■ **Save money.** You'll save on things such as stamps, stationery, and employee wages.

■ **Please your customers.** When things get busy you'll still be able to follow up with prospects quickly and stay in touch with customers. They won't feel ignored and that will help you build lasting relationships with them.

■ **Gain a competitive edge.** Automation will allow you to devote more time to things such as identifying golden opportunities, improving customer care, and researching new products, so you'll definitely stand out from your competitors.

■ **Find it easier to segment your target market** and separate prospects from customers. Automation makes it easy to divide groups of people by interests, responses, buying behaviors, and so on.

It's never been simpler, or more affordable, for business owners to maintain their competitive edge by using affordable and highly effective internet-based software designed to put their marketing communication on autopilot, especially for tasks such as:

- answering frequently asked questions regarding products and services
- delivering mini courses
- thanking members, guests, and customers
- following up with current customers and prospects
- managing e-mail lists
- tracking and measuring marketing campaign results
- confirming orders
- e-mailing call-in information for teleseminars
- processing credit cards in real time
- obtaining information regarding sales transactions
- segmenting prospects and customers into separate databases
- tracking affiliate activity
- accepting electronic checks
- measuring web site visitors, sales, and conversions

...and more!

As you can see, the list is extensive. And as a matter of fact, automating your site will play such an important role in your online success that I've devoted this entire chapter to helping you understand its benefits, uses, and step-by-step tips for setting it up. If you're like most online entrepreneurs you probably know very little about this technology; it may even sound intimidating. Yet once you learn more about its benefits, variety, and ease of use, you'll wonder how you ever did without it!

TYPES OF AUTOMATION

As the list in the preceding section indicates, there are many, many ways to automate your web site and there will be even more in years to come. At this point, however, it's more important to gain an understanding of the basics—that is, how automation programs work in general and ways online marketers can use them—rather than delve too deeply into specifics. Therefore, I have divided this chapter's content into three main parts—all having to do with one of the three main functions of automation, which are:

1. **Communication**
2. **Delivering products and taking money**
3. **Tracking and measuring marketing campaigns and sales**

PART 1: USING AUTOMATION TO COMMUNICATE EFFECTIVELY

Since building rapport with prospects and staying in touch with customers is vitally important to your online business, I'll begin with *autoresponders*—those wonderful tools that put your communication on autopilot. Although they may sound complex, autoresponders are simply tools that generate and send messages back to opt-in e-mail addresses. Depending upon the circumstances they can be sent once (single) or multiple times (sequential). Now let's take a look at each one separately.

SINGLE AUTORESPONDERS

Although I am a strong proponent of ongoing customer and prospect communication, there are times when you'll need to send out a single e-mail response each time one of your visitors opts in. Single autoresponders work well when you want to

- thank new customers right after their first sale
- deliver specific and/or time-sensitive information to groups such as conference call phone numbers, access codes, e-mail address, or web site URLs
- send live links for downloading pages, PDFs, audios files, and more

■ notify your e-mail list regarding one-time sales, volume discounts, and promotions—that is, get the word out to hundreds with one click of a mouse.

> ## "Good communication does not mean
>
> that you have to speak in perfectly formed sentences and paragraphs. It isn't about slickness. Simple and clear go a long way."
>
> —*John Kotter, Professor, Harvard Business School*

I recommend that you purchase an easy-to-use automation program with multiple features and flexibility (such as EasyWebAutomation.com, which I discuss in more detail later in this chapter). Regardless of the program you choose, however, you can set one up using the following very basic steps:

1. **Create your opt-in event.** Decide what you'll give in exchange for your visitors' name and e-mail address (e.g., special report, teleclass, newsletter, e-book, two-month free membership, etc.) when they visit your web site.

2. **Set up an autoresponder feed** that sends your opt-in responders' contact information to a database (a file folder within the software), which you'll create and name. This is easier than you would imagine with the technologies available today.

3. **Compose a message** that welcomes your opt-ins and includes the promised information.

As I said previously, there are times when using single autoresponders make sense, but most often you'll use them to send out series of scheduled messages to groups and individuals. Now let's move on to sequential autoresponders—your online marketing communication's automated workforce.

SEQUENTIAL AUTORESPONDERS

Sequential autoresponders are tools that help you send chunks of information (e.g., mini e-courses, weekly e-mail tips, reminders, etc.) to various, and differing, groups of people who have opted in to your e-mail list over a certain period of time. So, what's entailed in setting up sequential autoresponders? I've broken it down into five steps (which follow). You'll note that the steps are similar to the ones provided for single autoresponders, although there are some key differences.

Additionally, I use my own site as an example of how yours might look. Remember, these are very basic guidelines, so don't sweat the details! Your automation software will come with comprehensive directions.

Step 1: Decide What You Want to Deliver

Choose the type of information to include in your series of e-mails, such as an eight-part e-course on getting traffic to a web site, weekly dog-training tips, or daily inspirational quotes on a particular subject.

Step 2: Give Each E-Mail a Different Title

For example, here's how you might title your messages. Day one: "The Three Biggest Mistakes Online Marketers Make and How to Avoid Them;" day two: "The Two Things Online Marketers Should Do Every Day;" day three: "The Ins and Outs of Pay-Per-Click Campaigns," etc. Remember, once your visitors opt in to your list you can broadcast or e-mail them with relevant offers. Keep in mind, however, that they signed up for pertinent and valuable information, so don't risk becoming a pest by over-sending sales pitches. (Not only

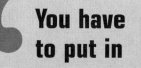

You have to put in many, many, many tiny efforts that nobody sees or appreciates before you achieve anything worthwhile."

—*Brian Tracy, author and motivational speaker*

will this annoy your recipients, but they may even ask to be removed from your mailing list.) Balance is everything.

If you'd like more exacting under-the-hood details for programming your database(s), you can view a video at www.EasyWebAutomationVideos.com.

Step 3: Craft Your E-mails

Begin your communication series by composing a letter that welcomes your respondents, reaffirms their wise choice, and generates anticipation over the wonderful content they'll soon receive. Then, once you create the message, set a delivery schedule and—bingo—it will continue being sent automatically, and you won't have to lift another finger!

Following are some quick tips for getting it right:

- Personalize your message. Give your e-mail a better chance of being read by using your recipients' names! This can be done simply by using merge codes, which automatically place specified data like first names into your messages.

- Advise your recipients to set up a folder to store the content you'll be sending for future use. That way, they'll be likely to refer back to it at a later date (and not delete it!). If you include an exclamation point (!) before the folder name, it will bring it to the top of their e-mail list.

- Provide directions for adding your e-mail address to their "safe sender" e-mail list. Make sure that your e-mails get through your recipients' spam filter—a must, given today's spamming problems.

- Tell them exactly what they're going to receive. Reiterate the wonderful content that will be coming their way.

- Include an active direct link to one of your web pages that contains each week's content chunk. Make sure it's visible and they know what to do.

Figure 7-2 is an example of one of my own e-mail letters. You can use it as a guide for developing yours. Please note that it is short and simple; remember, your visitors are busy. It also contains two links to my web site—one very close to the top and one at the bottom—and the content section highlights the course's benefits.

Step 4: Program and Schedule E-Mail Deliveries

Once you've got your letter ready, it's time to select and program your series. When you start your sequential communication series, make sure to send your messages out regularly and consistently. As you can see in the screenshot for my own mini-course (see Figure 7-3), they're scheduled according to intervals, not dates. For instance, you'll notice that the first e-mail has 0 days delay. This means that it will be sent (and received) immediately. The next four e-mails will

FIGURE 7-2. E-MAIL LETTER

Hi, < first name >!

I wanted to reach out to you personally to say thanks and welcome you to my recently updated internet marketing multimedia mini course. I've worked hard to ensure that the content is fresh (I've included loads of new audios and videos) and know you'll find my up-to-the-minute tips useful and actionable—even if you've already taken this course!

In a hurry? No problem. Simply go to www.OnlineMarketingSuperstars. com/mini/one.htm to get Part One, which includes great information including audios and an informative video. Then get ready to learn:

■ The most effective ways to drive traffic to your web site

■ How to increase your conversion ratio by up to 300%

■ The five things you absolutely need to know in order to create products that sell

■ How to double—or even triple—your opt-in list

■ The most profitable ways to use audio on your web site

■ One-page versus portal web sites: the pros and cons of each

…and much more!

Are you ready to receive tips from the world's most successful online marketers? If so, click here: www.OnlineMarketingSuperstars.com/mini/one.htm

To Your Success,

Mitch Meyerson

Founder, Guerrilla Marketing Coaching Certification Program and author of *Success Secrets of the Online Marketing Superstars*

FIGURE 7-3. Sequential Autoresponder Interval List

CREATE NEW AUTORESPONDER | INHERIT AUTORESPONDER | TRACK AUTORESPONDER REPORTS

Autoresponder Message	Days Delay	Message Type	Update Message
<$today$> Online Marketing Superstars Mi...- 0 days delay	0	Text	EDIT | DELETE
<$today$> Online Superstars Part 2: Marl...- 3 days delay	3	Text	EDIT | DELETE
<$today$> Online Superstars Part 3: The ...- 7 days delay	7	Text	EDIT | DELETE
<$today$> Online Superstars Part 4: Yani...- 10 days delay	10	Text	EDIT | DELETE
<$today$> Online Superstars Part 5: The ...- 13 days delay	13	Text	EDIT | DELETE
Online Marketing Superstars - Your Speci...- 15 days delay	15	Text	EDIT | DELETE
My Most-Asked Online Marketing Question....- 17 days delay	17	Text	EDIT | DELETE
<$today$> Online Superstars Part 6: Mast...- 21 days delay	21	Text	EDIT | DELETE
<$today$> Online Superstars Part 7: Core...- 25 days delay	25	Text	EDIT | DELETE
<$today$> Online Superstars Part 8 - How...- 28 days delay	28	Text	EDIT | DELETE
<$today$> Online Marketing Superstars Ba...- 33 days delay	33	Text	EDIT | DELETE

go out 3, 7, 10, and 13 days, respectively. That pattern will continue until all 11 e-mails are delivered.

That's basically all there is to it! It's probably not as difficult at you thought, is it? And remember, this is just one example, so don't hesitate to use your imagination when you set up your own. And just think: once you've completed your program, you can stay in touch with your targeted prospects and customers often, regularly, and most importantly, automatically!

MY STORY

When I decided to write my first marketing book, *Success Secrets of the Online Marketing Superstars* (Chicago: Dearborn, 2005), a compilation of personal interviews I conducted with 24 of the world's most successful e-commerce marketers, I recognized I had a lot of work ahead of me before I'd ever see it in a bookstore. Yet I realized early on that the content I was collecting was perfect for a mini course even before the book was written.

Now here's where it gets fun. I used my shopping cart and autoresponder system to create a sequential autoresponder-based mini course that contained audio excerpts of the interviews I had completed (with permission from the

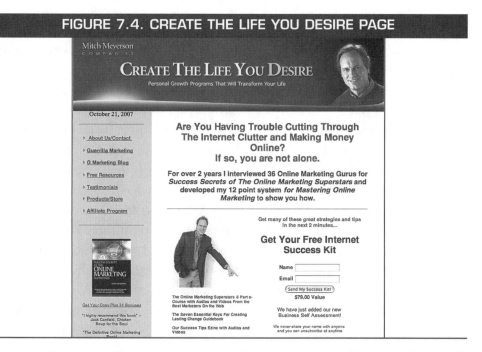

FIGURE 7.4. CREATE THE LIFE YOU DESIRE PAGE

experts, of course). Each e-mail featured one superstar who provided solid and actionable tips.

I set up a professional looking web page explaining what my customers would get and featuring all the benefits of the content in the audios. Within one year I had more than 16,000 sign-ups! I subsequently used this list to mail announcements for my book when it was completed.

I still use this strategy to build my e-mail lists. The screen shot from my web site www.MitchMeyerson.com (Figure 7-4), shows one of my opt-in pages. Note that I offer a combination of an eight-part multimedia mini course with audio excerpts from *Success Secrets of the Online Marketing Superstars* and a PDF from one of my other books, *The Six Keys to Creating the Life You Desire*. Visitors who opt in also receive a free subscription to my online newsletter.

Once you get really good at this process, you should consider creating autoresponders to get customers to consume products that they have purchased as well other offers and services. When you're ready, you'll want to set up targeted sublists, which I discuss in the next section.

CREATE TARGETED SUBLISTS

As I've said over and over again throughout this book, your online business will be more successful if you don't try to appeal to the masses. Rather, you should carve out niches within your industry by identifying small pockets of hard core prospects in narrow subgroups, particularly the ones who are actively seeking your products or services. For instance, you'd probably have far more luck reaching out to French poodle owners (and it might even be better if they were miniature French poodle owners) than dog owners!

I'm reiterating this now because it's important that you keep it in mind while you're developing your opt-in offers. While it's okay to offer one or more unrelated products or services, do not recommend all of them to everyone on your list! For example, you wouldn't want to send an invitation for a mini course on tactics for teaching your cat to use a litter box to bird enthusiasts!

If you sell multiple products or services that appeal to different audiences, you should create a targeted sublist for each. Since I operate more than one web site with dissimilar content (marketing, psychology, and music), I'd be lost if I couldn't create sublists easily.

Figure 7-5 shows a few of my own sublists. At this point I have 75 different prospect groups, which are categorized based on various criteria. As you'll see, some of my opt-ins chose my Success Tips e-zine, others downloaded my Six

FIGURE 7.5. Autoresponder Sublist

Autoresponder Name ⇕	Msgs in Series ⇕	Unique Clients ⇕
!!Success Tips Ezine	0	28846
!GM Toolkit Sampler	5	2042
!GMC Next 2004	1	210
!Michael Gerber Teleclinic	1	735
!Mitch's Songs	1	294
!OMS 2004	13	6734
!Online Marketing Superstars 8 Week E-course	9	9821
!Six Keys	7	2198

Keys' psychology freebie, many requested information on my next Guerrilla Marketing Coach Certification Program, and still others wanted to hear my songs at www.Mitchsongs.com.

The power of these sublists is that I can send individual announcements to a targeted group of people who are interested in a specific topic. That way I don't send marketing tips to someone who asked for songs! That means each mailing is relevant to the recipient, which results in higher response rates. Even if you're starting out with one list, it's a great idea to get in the habit of creating sublists.

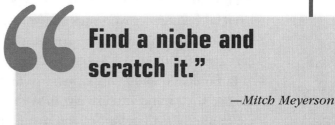

Find a niche and scratch it."

—*Mitch Meyerson*

PART 2: TAKING MONEY ONLINE

If you're developing a traditional e-commerce web site and want to remain competitive you'll need to set up easy, convenient, and secure online payment options such as credit cards (VISA, MasterCard, American Express, Discover, etc.), electronic checks, and PayPal for your customers. And even if you're not planning to accept online payments, you should still be aware of the process involved in making that happen for several reasons.

First, things change. Who knows what you'll be doing in several years? Second, you may want to add supplemental products and/or services that are more appropriate for online payments. And lastly, as a convenience to your clients, you may want to add a bill payment option to your site.

Trust me, automating and streamlining your customers' online payments will save you tons of time and stress. But before I get into ways to automate this process, let's step back a minute to review the basics.

STEP 1: SET UP A BANK ACCOUNT

If you haven't done so already, visit your favorite local bank and open a business checking account. Once you've set it up, you can deposit payments from your merchant or PayPal account into it.

STEP 2: SET UP YOUR SHOPPING CART

Simply put, *shopping carts* are the cyberspace versions of the ones in stores! Used by millions of web sites all over the world, they allow customers to act just as they would in a brick-and-mortar store: They can place things in their cart and take them out as often as they'd like before purchasing.

But unlike traditional shoppers, online consumers are much more likely to change their mind and leave your web site without purchasing. Although the exact numbers depend on whom you ask, shopping cart desertions are estimated to be as high as 85 percent.

What is the reason for this unfortunate situation? The simple answer is that many people get cold feet when faced with handing over their personal and financial information online, even though it is a very secure payment method. (Shopping carts use digital converters that encrypt information and make it nearly impossible for anyone else to access it.)

So, in order to remove this daunting obstacle, leave nothing to chance and make sure that people feel safe and comfortable submitting payments in your shopping cart area.

Following are some quick tips for decreasing your shopping cart abandonment:

- **Reiterate your site's security features.** It doesn't matter that they're considered standard elements today. Take time to reassure your customers again with pleasant and well-placed copy, audio, or video.

- **Brand order pages.** Choose a system that allows you to customize your order form and payment pages with your logo and graphics and lets you change elements (e.g., colors, fonts, sizes, etc.) easily.

- **Sound enthusiastic!** Write, "Yes! I can't wait to receive..." This starts the purchasing process off on a great note.

- **Restate and emphasize your strong guarantee.** Reverse the customers' risk—it's very reassuring.

- **Summarize your offer's strongest benefits.** This reminds people why they got to the order page in the first place.

- **Include all of your contact information.** Clearly display your phone number, mailing and e-mail addresses, and name.

- **Restate your discount, special terms, and detailed shipping information.** The more information prospects have, the better they'll feel.

- **Use audio and/or video, if possible.** Seeing and/or hearing you will increase your customers' comfort level, especially if you're reinforcing your guarantees, privacy policy, and so forth.

PAYPAL

Want a quick way to begin taking online payments? If so, consider setting up a PayPal account (go to www.PayPal.com) and you'll be good to go in a matter of minutes. Although PayPal can function alone, it works best as an added option for your customers who already have PayPal accounts.

For a small charge, PayPal will process payments on your behalf and deposit the money—almost instantly—into your bank account, without having to set up a separate merchant account. At the time of this writing, PayPal's transaction fees were 1.9-2.9 percent of the total dollar amount purchased plus $.30 (USD).

Although you can open a PayPal account quicker and less expensively (and your customers can also use any major credit card) it is not quite as flexible as a merchant account. For instance, all payments will be deposited into your PayPal account, which means you'll have to transfer the funds to your checking or savings account. Also, it doesn't allow you to accept credit card payments over the phone. If you'd like more details on opening a merchant account, try visiting www.EasyWebMerchant.com.

MERCHANT ACCOUNTS

It's never been easier to open up an online merchant account, which allows businesses to accept credit cards as well as other forms of payment. You can apply for one through an online merchant account provider. It usually takes several days for your account to become active. Some local banks also provide merchant accounts; however, the majority of them deal primarily with brick-and-mortar retailers.

Fundamentally, merchant accounts serve as payment gateways for businesses and enable the transfer of funds from the buyers' credit cards or checking accounts to sellers' checking accounts. When choosing a merchant account provider for your online business, be sure that you'll have the ability to do the following:

■ Process credit cards and checks through a virtual terminal using any computer with an internet connection. It should be available around the clock in a secure, real-time environment.

■ Seamlessly integrate with an online shopping cart and e-commerce solution that will enable you to take orders through your web site.

■ Charge clients, students, and members monthly, quarterly, or annually for fees and dues. Your customers' credit cards or checking accounts will be charged automatically, you'll receive a notice, and they'll get automatic e-mail receipts.

■ Most importantly, use multiple levels of security that can identify potential fraudulent charges to protect you from any losses.

Your provider should enable you to do all the above, as well as offering you and your business the support you need to succeed. Be aware that there are one-time, and ongoing, fees associated with maintaining a merchant account. Again, they vary, but can include penalties for not reaching monthly minimums, an initial set-up charge, transaction and address verification fees, and more. I advise you to compare several providers' policies before choosing one.

PART 3: TRACKING AND MEASURING MARKETING CAMPAIGNS AND SALES

As I discussed in Chapter 6, it's imperative that you track and measure all of your key web site metrics, such as:

■ **Traffic**: the number of people that visit your site; the number of times your average visitor returns; the number of pages they view on your site; etc.

■ **Conversions**: the number of visitors who opt in to your mailing list, convert to sales, and your average visitor value

■ **Marketing Communications:** the effectiveness of ad types, copy, headlines, delivery vehicles, etc.

If you don't keep track of these factors, you'll never know what's working and what isn't. And today's technology makes it really simple to set up and obtain all the information you need automatically.

AD TRACKERS

One of the biggest challenges with sending marketing e-mails is finding out how many people actually clicked through to your web page and viewed your promotional offer. And if you don't have this information, you'll never know what you should continue, amend, or erase. Once again, you can't improve what you don't measure. However, this problem is easily solved using ad trackers, which are primarily designed to track marketing campaigns and promotions. Even better, they're simple to set up and operate.

There are many types of ad trackers available, and they all work pretty much the same. First, you'll purchase some ad-tracking software—either a stand-alone program or one that's included with your shopping cart. The advantage of using one that's integrated into your shopping cart is that it tracks your click-throughs and calculates your sales and opt-in statistics as well (see Figure 7-6).

Next, you'll decide what promotion, ad, or event you'd like to measure. For example, let's say you sent your e-mail list an offer for special pricing on one of your products. However, instead of providing a link directly to your sales page, you set up an ad tracker, which created a new link but still got your visitors to the same destination, and documented every time someone clicked on the ad tracker link. Even better, you'd also know how many people actually purchased your product or service or opted in to your list.

Figure 7-6 is a screenshot of an ad-tracking report I used in the past. As you can see, it provides information on three separate e-mail campaigns and lets me quickly view my most important metrics, such as how many people

■ clicked through to my web page

■ opted in to my list (leads)

■ bought my product.

FIGURE 7-6. Ad Tracking Report

Track Your Ad Campaigns

Campaign Name	Select	Clicks	Leads	Lead-Click Conversion	Sales Amount	# Sales	Click-Sale Conversion	Visitor Value
*GMARKETINGCOACH-TOOLKIT	⊟	405	25	6.2%	$1183.00	6	1.5%	$2.92 per click
*GMC Coach Cert- Top Link Dec 1 2003	⊟	577	68	11.8%	$5305.00	8	1.4%	$9.19 per click
*GMC Ezine -OMSbook 2/20	⊟	1054	232	22%	$1358.00	14	1.3%	$1.29 per click
*GMCCert to 48people Dec2	⊟	25	0	0%	$2125.00	2	8%	$85.00 per click
*GMCezine - Terry Dean/Mitch 28 day Internet Prog	⊟	288	10	3.5%	$632.00	8	2.8%	$2.19 per click
*OMS newsletter tracking	⊟	556	39	7%	$802.00	8	1.4%	$1.44 per click

Additionally, it tells me the average revenue generated per click-through (visitor value).

The two most important things you'll learn are how compelling your copy and offer are and what actions your prospects took as a result. Additionally, if your visitor value metric is strong, you'll find it easier to attract valuable joint venture partners. Why? Because facts don't lie; others will be able to see for themselves exactly how much money they're likely to make if they send out a similar e-mail promotion for your product to their list. This is more critical than ever because successful online marketers are increasingly, and understandably, protective of overmailing to their coveted e-mail lists.

MY CHOICE

As you can tell, I'm a strong believer in the power of automating web sites and can't imagine anyone going into this business without a good system. I've developed multiple internet businesses since 1999 so I've had the opportunity to experience an e-commerce business without automation. It's not fun or cost-effective, and it doesn't generate profits. And, since there are so many affordable, easy-to-use solutions, there's no good reason for doing without.

After much research I purchased a system that is now called EasyWebAutomation (visit www.EasyWebAutomation.com), which quickly became my internet business's best friend. And although I had no idea what I was getting myself into, I followed the directions in the straightforward tutorials and had my first site on autopilot in no time. The most important thing to remember is that you absolutely must automate your web site if you're serious about building and sustaining a thriving

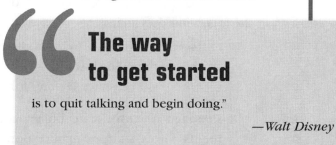

The way to get started is to quit talking and begin doing."

—*Walt Disney*

online business. And even though I'm partial to this system, there are lots of others to choose from. You'll find it quick and easy to locate other automation programs by logging on to your favorite search engine (e.g., www.google.com, www.msn.com, www.yahoo.com) and typing logical keywords such as "automation software," "autoresponders," or "automation solutions" into the search box.

Regardless of which one you choose, make sure you select an automation program that provides the following:

- unlimited autoresponders and e-mail broadcasting capabilities (with no cost per e-mail)

- support for managing sales channels, marketing campaigns, and ads

- updating, so you never outgrow it

- a one-stop solution that integrates all of your automation needs; allows you to track and manage lists and money; and lets you communicate with prospects and customers

- uncomplicated set up and programming—you shouldn't have to download or install anything

- flexibility—allowing people to buy all kinds of products, especially instant downloads (e.g., white papers, special reports, e-books, software, etc.)

- ad tracking, so you can find out what is working and what's not

- excellent customer support to help you in the early set-up stages.

WEB WORK: YOUR INTERACTIVE ADVENTURE

Since time is your most valuable resource, look for ways to use it wisely. In addition to the automation tools I've discussed in this chapter, how many of the following do you use?

- **Outsource.** Don't try to do it all—you'll usually end up wasting money as well as time! For instance, why spend two hours changing your car's oil when you can have it done for less than $20?

- **Prepare ahead**. Create boilerplated marketing communication, documents, forms, and/or e-mail responses before you need them. As the saying goes, the best time to fix a roof is when the sun's shining. Keep relevant content in an easy-to-find file and use all, or parts, of it as needed.

- **Bank online.** You can pay bills, check your bank balance, and transfer funds quickly and securely. Also, consider setting up automatic payments for regular expenses. You'll be amazed at the amount of time this saves.

- **Automate.** Provide automatic payment options for your customers. Invoices are time-consuming to develop and costly to mail, so if appropriate, consider setting up an automatic payment system.

- **Consolidate communications.** Answer e-mails and phone calls once or twice a day only. If you're in the habit of answering e-mails or returning phone calls whenever you receive them, resist the urge (unless of course, there's a good reason for doing so immediately). You'll find it's less distracting and more efficient to respond to several at once.

- **Organize your work space.** If you're like many people, you waste a lot of time looking for papers ("I know I put it in a safe place… how far could it have gone?"), computer documents, rubber bands, staples, and the like. You'll save yourself a ton of time and stress by getting rid of unnecessary clutter and paper and reorganizing your computer's documents and filing system.

- **Plan tomorrow today.** Take ten minutes out right before you quit work for the day to prepare a prioritized to-do list for the next day. Then, when you're back in your office, work first on those tasks that you can complete in two minutes or less. This will make it easier to get started and you'll feel better knowing you've crossed some things off your list quickly. Then start working on your most imperative responsibilities next, in order of importance.

- **Use tools** such as Microsoft Outlook or Apple's Entourage to help manage your e-mails. You can easily set up rules for managing and filing e-mails automatically.

- **Use templates.** Why reinvent the wheel? Look for fill-in-the-blank samples, examples, and patterns (i.e., templates) when you want to compose letters, forms, work proposals, employee guidelines, organizational charts, invoices, and so on. For more information on my templates, visit www. OnlineMarketingTemplates.com.

- **Teach.** Think of strong information you have (or can find) that will educate your target audience. Put it down on paper and place the content into four to eight logical sections (about two paragraphs each). Consider developing these into your own e-mail based mini-course.

- **Review this chapter** and select the best ways to automate your online business.

- **Get more details** on automating your site by viewing a video at: www.EasyWebAutomationVideos.com

- **Use PayPal.** If you're ready, and it's appropriate, set up PayPal account at www.PayPal.com. It's easy.

- **Learn more** about setting up a merchant account at www. EasyWebMerchant.com

CHAPTER 7 REMINDERS

Before moving on to Chapter 8, "Multimedia: The Key to Increasing Your Impact," let's take a minute to review the most important lessons learned from this chapter:

■ If you want to be truly successful online and have time to enjoy it, you must automate.

■ Setting up automated systems allows you to set it and forget it. You can run your business 24/7/365, no matter where you're located!

■ If you'd like more information on the benefits of automation, tips for automating your site, PayPal, merchant's accounts, or ad trackers, simply go to my web site at www. MasteringOnlineMarketing.com. You'll find free up-to-the-minute blogs, advice, articles, templates, and more.

■ Automate your offline mailings from your computer. Visit www. EasyWeb Cards.com.

> ## " As you begin to take action...
>
> toward the fulfillment of your goals and dreams, you must realize that not every action will be perfect. Not every action will produce the desired result. Not every action will work. Making mistakes, getting it almost right, and experimenting to see what happens are all part of the process of eventually getting it right."
>
> —*Jack Canfield, American motivational speaker and author*

MULTIMEDIA

Increasing Your Impact using Audio, Video, and Conferencing

In this chapter you'll learn

- *all about multimedia—what it means and how to use it*

- *ways to use audio and video to enhance your visitors' experiences*

- *why teleconferencing and web conferencing will help you build relationships with customers and colleagues*

- *what's ahead in multimedia*

...and much more.

> **The world is but a canvas to the imagination."**
>
> *—Henry David Thoreau,*
> *American author, naturalist, and philosopher*

Record numbers of people, young and old, are taking advantage of new technology (e.g., cell phones, MP3 players, and other mobile devices), increased broadband connectivity, and the groundbreaking formatting of web sites such as www.MySpace.com and www.YouTube.com to obtain information on-demand faster and more conveniently than ever before.

Additionally, the internet's recent upgrade to Web 2.0 functionality (see Chapter 11) has made it the go-to channel for people looking for memorable, story-based multimedia messaging and allowed online marketers to add these elements to their sites quickly, simply, and affordably.

Although people use the term *multimedia* to describe many different communication delivery vehicles that are used to entertain or enlighten people (e.g., animation, print, radio, TV, graphics, interactive programs, etc.), I'll focus on three forms of *active electronic audiovisuals*—audios, videos, and web conferencing—and provide insights into using them effectively to leverage your online business. I strongly believe that the benefits for including customer-centric multimedia elements on your web site are so forceful and undeniable that failing to do so is a huge mistake. You'll receive many paybacks when you add audio and/or video elements to your e-commerce site. For example, they'll help you

- **Jump-start the relationship-building process.** Because you'll be engaging multiple senses, your visitors will become more emotionally involved right from the beginning.

- **Appear far more professional and credible.** Using multiple interfaces in this way suggests that you're on the cutting edge and more proficient than most.

- **Educate your audience quickly and effectively.** A picture is worth a thousand words! For instance, you can demonstrate how to use your products, trouble-shoot technical problems, set up new service, and the like.

Before beginning, keep in mind that multimedia content has to be delivered in the way your audience wants it. It must be

- **Available 24/7.** Using the power of the internet, you can now reach a global market anytime.

- **On demand.** The days of scheduled entertainment are over. TiVo and iPods allow people to view what they want when they want it.

- **Two-way.** Making it as interactive as possible enhances your users' experience and builds rapport—keys for making them want to return to your site over and over again.

PART 1: WEB AUDIO SIMPLIFIED

Adding audio—music and voiceovers—to your web site can significantly reduce the time it takes to build relationships with your prospects and customers and may even help you establish and maintain closer connections with them. Why? People are more attentive and emotionally engaged when they use more than one of their senses (touching, seeing, smelling, hearing, and tasting) or use the same sense in multiple ways (e.g., hear voices and music or see words and pictures) to decipher a message. This is particularly relevant when the vehicle allows the communicator to convey meaningful thoughts, concepts, and feelings. That's why it's easier to get to know and trust others when you can see and/or hear them rather than simply read their written text on a page. And let's face it, enthusiasm is contagious; your web site visitors will become far more excited about your products and/or services if they can hear you, or someone else, describe their benefits passionately, vividly, clearly, and honestly.

And although this may sound a little silly at first, audio will also help your prospects view you as real flesh-and-blood person rather than a cyberspace stranger—a very important requirement for building lasting relationships, particularly given the impersonal nature of the internet.

WAYS TO USE WEB AUDIO

There are many ways to use web audio effectively. The method you choose will depend upon your site type and your product and/or service offerings. However, here are some ideas:

- **Testimonials.** Let your visitors hear recorded testimonials from happy customers. Listen to a sample at www.MitchMeyerson.com/consulting.htm.

- **Welcome Messages.** There's no better time to introduce yourself to new prospects than when they first visit your site. So greet them warmly and enthusiastically and punctuate particular points of interest.

- **Guarantees.** Help alleviate any lingering doubts would-be customers may have by reassuring them that purchasing from you is essentially risk free.

- **Music.** Use it to energize, soothe, demo CDs, or just have some fun. For a sample visit www.MitchSongs.com.

- **Teleseminar Recordings and Archiving.** Record and upload tele-seminars so students who miss sessions can listen to them later on. This also works wonderfully for training sites where streamable on-demand audios are highly sought after.

- **Audio postcards.** Send your associates, prospects, and customers an e-mail link to a web page containing your pre-recorded audio message. This is great for special offers, holiday greetings, or reminders. The e-mail may include links to your products and services as well (check out www.InstantFlashAudio.com).

- **Audio e-Courses.** Instead of offering your prospects a sequential text e-course, consider enhancing it with audio. For example, record one that your visitors can download onto their MP3 player or iPods; that way they can listen to your valuable tips on any device.

WHAT ARE THE MOST ACCEPTED WEB AUDIO FORMATS?

Although there are a number of audio formats available on the internet, I will discuss the two that have become the worldwide standard: MP3 and Flash. Here's a simple overview on how they work:

The MP3 format compresses very large audio files (like the ones that are on CDs) into much smaller ones so that they're easier to upload onto the internet. (Although it's a complex process in which certain frequencies are deleted, it is not necessary to understand the details in order to use it effectively.) The good news is that you'll barely notice the difference in sound quality between an

MP3 and a CD played over the internet because most computer speakers are not robust enough to pick up the smaller nuances. In addition, since most web audio is voice only—or voice with background music—the MP3 format works just fine.

Flash, on the other hand, is the closest thing to a foolproof audio (and video) delivery system. Originally created by Macromedia (now Adobe), it is embedded in every major browser. This means that 99 percent of your visitors will be able to use it without problems. And given today's short attention spans, you don't want to frustrate potential customers by having them download a player in order to listen to your audio.

Music produces a kind of pleasure that human nature cannot do without."

—*Confucius, Chinese philosopher*

Additionally, you can convert your MP3 audio into a Flash format, which will help create sound that's more consistent and allow for instant playback. Visit web sites such as www.InstantFlashAudio.com and www.AudioAcrobat.com if you want to quickly convert your MP3 files (they even have cool little play buttons and audio postcards).

ADDING AUDIO TO YOUR WEB SITE

Thanks to affordable, state-of-the-art technology, adding audio to your web site is a snap. You'll just need the following software and few simple tools and you'll be good to go:

- **A microphone.** You can buy a good mid-range, USB-cabled microphone at most electronics stores (do not purchase the less expensive ones that plug into your sound card—you'll be disappointed in the quality). Plug it into your computer's USB port (every computer manufactured within the last three to five years comes equipped with multiple ports) and wait a bit until the computer automatically recognizes the new hardware (you'll receive an alert when it's ready). Although any microphone will suffice,

I like the simplicity (true plug-and-play capability), comfort (ear buds), and clarity of the headset models.

- **Recording software.** In order to record and upload your audio, you'll need to purchase software. The good news is that there are several really excellent, and inexpensive, choices on the internet. I strongly suggest that you find one that provides simple instructions, one-button recording and saving capabilities to an MP3 or computer hard drive. Check out SoundForge for PCs or Garageband (included in iLife) for Macs.

  One of my favorites is a small piece of software you can purchase online. It is very easy to use and will have you making professional web audio in a snap. For more information and/or to hear it in action, go to www.FiveMinuteWebAudio.com. For a complete line of audio and video recording solutions for the internet, visit www.OnlineMarketing Superstore.com.

- **Uploading software.** Once you've recorded and saved your audio message, you'll upload it onto your web page using *file transfer protocol (FTP) software,* which allows you to transfer files from your computer hard drive to your web hosting server (where your web site is stored and available on the internet). To create and modify web pages you will need additional software such as Microsoft FrontPage, Adobe Dreamweaver, or another leading development program (which all include FTP capabilities). Again, if this is outside of your comfort area, ask your web developer for help.

As you set up your audio, keep in mind that your visitors will be listening through many different types of speakers—big, small, top-of-the-line, and bottom. That's why it is important that you optimize your recordings for the lowest-quality

Uploading Audio

The quickest way to upload audio is through the admin section of blogging web sites such as www.WordPress.com. These great tools allow you to add multimedia—audio, video, Word documents, and so on—to your site seamlessly, you don't need to know a thing about programming or download any special software. You simply browse your computer's hard drive for the file, select it, and hit Submit.

speakers so you won't lose listeners. And since the vast majority of online shoppers (more than 70 percent) connect to the internet via broadband, the problems associated with dial-up audio delivery, such as inconsistent quality and reliability, have all but disappeared.

PODCASTS

Podcasting combines the ease of blogging with the fun of hosting your very own radio or TV show. Today, it is used by companies of all sizes—from media mega-giants to solo professionals—that are looking for new ways to differentiate themselves in the marketplace.

Podcasting Basics

Essentially, podcasts are recorded audio and/or video files that can be downloaded automatically into multiple devices—iPods, desktops, computers, MP3 players, and so on. They allow people to subscribe to one or more series such as radio and TV shows, internet videos, or even someone recording audio from their home office. Then, when new episodes are posted they are automatically downloaded and can be enjoyed whenever and wherever the subscriber chooses.

Following are some of the benefits of podcasting. They allow for:

- **Time Shifting.** Like their predecessor, the VCR, podcasts allow viewers to download on-demand media quickly and easily, something they've come to expect on the internet.

- **Place Shifting.** Podcasts can be put anywhere. You can download them on to multiple portable devices like iPods, MP3 players, and other video devices.

- **Consumer Production.** Podcasts are great examples of citizen journalism media formats. Affordable technology now makes it possible for almost anyone to produce them.

- **Quick Access.** As worldwide broadband deployment continues to grow, media files will be quickly downloaded and enjoyed by more people around the globe.

If you're looking for podcasts or would like more information, try these sites:

- www.iTunes.com
- www.Odeo.com
- www.PodcastAlley.com
- www.IndiePodder.org
- www.PodcastPickle.com

Getting Started

In order to create a podcast, you'll need to master three simple skills:

1. **Recording audio.** There are many options for recording audio; from rudimentary to sophisticated, and everything in between. As you probably expect, the quality of your finished product will depend in large part on the type of hardware and software you use.

2. **Uploading audio.** Once your audio is recorded, you'll need to use an FTP program or podcasting software to upload it from your hard drive to the internet.

3. **Posting the audio.** After your audio is uploaded, you'll add it to your podcast files. Most people use blog software such as WordPress or TypePad to send files to subscribers and manage their podcasts.

PART 2: WEB VIDEO SIMPLIFIED

There is no better way to make a great first impression than by looking people in the eye and speaking to them with warmth, passion, and conviction. After all, this is what great salespeople have been doing for centuries. They understand that profitable sales have as much to do with establishing emotional connections as they do with outstanding features and benefits.

Web videos afford you—or someone else—the opportunity to combine words, tone, body language, and facial expressions to convey meaningful information about you, your company, and your products and services. And if they are composed sincerely, your passion will shine, your confidence will stand out, your genuine interest in others will become clear, and your commitment to offer superior products and service will be obvious.

If not, and you're just doing it for the money, you'll be found out. Never underestimate the intelligence of online consumers.

WHAT SHOULD YOU DO IF YOU'RE UNCOMFORTABLE ON CAMERA?

Creating an effective video—one that helps you grow and maintain positive relationships with your prospects and customers—begins with conducting a candid assessment of your presentation skills, because you don't want your video to hurt, rather than help, you. Let's face it; some of us should just not be in front of a camera for a variety of reasons. If you suspect that you fall in that category, ask a family member or friend to provide you with honest feedback and suggestions for ways you can improve. If you choose to avoid the camera, you can still do such things as:

> " **If a picture says a thousand words,** videos say a million. There's no substitution for eyeball-to-eyeball contact and web video is the electronic equivalent of meeting face-to-face with each and every one of your web site's visitors."
>
> —*Mike Stewart, internet marketing expert (www.InternetVideoGuy.com)*

- **Make someone else the star.** Ask an articulate, attractive, and enthusiastic friend or colleague to be your on-camera spokesperson.

- **Do a voice-over narration.** Create a strong audio script, read and record it, and add it to a simple video.

- **Create a slide show.** Use PowerPoint or a similar program to create an appealing presentation using bullet points, still images, and narration.

- **Demonstrate a product or showcase a service.** Nobody has to see your face—how about just your hands?

WHAT IS THE MOST UNIVERSALLY ACCEPTED VIDEO FORMAT?

Simply put, Flash. It is the format used by YouTube as well many other giant portals on the web. At least for the foreseeable future, it is the format that your web site visitors will have the most successful experience with whether they are on a PC or Mac.

Adding Video to Your Web Site

Like audio, MP3 web videos are also compressed when formatted for the internet, therefore it is not necessary to purchase expensive camera equipment because the finer nuances and fidelity will be lost anyway. Your goal should be to create a video that's interesting, compelling, informative, and entertaining, so don't worry about making it ready for prime time—leave that to TV professionals. However, do consider using your video as a substitute for TV and/or radio ads. You can achieve equal, or better, results for far less money.

All you really need is the following:

- **An inexpensive, digital camcorder.** If you're looking for an excellent selection of web-compatible equipment, visit Best Buy or Circuit City.

- **A decent microphone.** Again, you don't need top of the line, just something that is reliable and has reasonably good audio quality. And since most cameras come with microphones already installed, you probably won't have to purchase one separately.

- **Editing Software.** There are plenty of video and audio editing software packages available, both high end and shareware. Try Windows Movie Maker or the Macintosh equivalent, iMovie. For hardware and software options, visit www.OnlineMarketingSuperstore.com.

- **Uploading Software.** As with audio, you can use software like MS Frontpage, Adobe Dreamweaver, or Contribute to place your video on a web page and a file transfer program (FTP) to upload it.

As I said earlier, if this sounds like something you'd rather not take on, ask your web developer to take care of it for you.

WAYS TO USE VIDEO TO INCREASE REVENUES

Since your videos will be fascinating and informative, people will pay attention to them—an online marketer's dream. So, why not seize the moment and use this creative vehicle to help improve your bottom line? Here's how:

- **Tell them where to get more.** Always put your web site's URL in your movie, at the end, so folks know where to find you. Alternatively, place the URL in small semi-transparent text in the lower right-hand corner of your screen and have it run throughout (just as TV networks do with their logos during prime-time shows).

- **Be consistent.** Like everything else on the internet, regularity pays. It's better to create smaller, enjoyable videos more often than longer blockbusters every once in a while.

- **Create new, video-based products.** Distinguish yourself from the pack by creating a teleseminar or e-course with online video content. While you may not see immediate results, you can earn serious money over time.

- **Add video to your products.** Boost your products' and services' perceived value by packaging them with a video. For example, create DVDs from an instructional video or stream it from a password-protected area on your site.

YouTube

More and more people—young and old—are jumping on the internet's video bandwagon as evidenced by the tens of thousands of visitors to Google's recently purchased web site www.YouTube.com each day. Fueled by the Web's 2.0 social interaction concept and technological advances (see Chapter 11), novices and experts alike are adding their own videos to share ideas, entertain, demonstrate products, connect with others, and much more. And since access to the site is free and uploading a video is simple, it's a wonderful vehicle for practicing and honing your video skills.

Even better, YouTube technology utilizes a keyword generated interface (i.e. their videos are categorized using keywords or phrases so visitors can find videos on specific topics), which can result in an increase in targeted traffic to your web site *if you make sure viewers know how to find you* (e.g., mention it specifically in the video, find a URL that's really, really easy for your viewers to remember, and have a keyword-based user name like mine—InternetCoach).

Lights, Camera, Action!

Online marketing superstar, Rob Schultz, a specialist in web audio and viral video, offers five tips for making great videos for the web. You don't need to be Spielberg to be successful. By harnessing the following decidedly low-tech principles, you can vault the success of your own video:

- **Capture your audience's attention.** You have 15 to 30 seconds (tops!) to interest viewers in your online video. Give your audience a reason to stay right off the bat, or they won't hang around long. Video is not about telling your prospects everything about you. It's simply about capturing their attention, and then getting them to take the next step. So capture their fancy immediately, then let them know where and how to get more of you.

- **Entertain your audience.** Folks are expecting much more from their web experience. So find a way to deliver your message in laser form, in a highly entertaining way. Give them a ride (not a pitch) and chances are they'll hop on board.

- **It's about your viewers, not about you.** Yes, I know you have an impressive background, I just don't care. I care about me: my success, my relationships, my financial security, my ideal life. Your video should help viewers see themselves and their goals as the stars of your movie, let them know you understand them, and that you've got their solution.

- **Stealth marketing.** Don't pontificate! If you want to turn people off, tell them about your five-step process for nirvana. If you want to excite people (and my guess is that's why you're using video) give them a vivid, emotional, compelling vision of nirvana, and then invite them in.

- **Take a stand.** A wise person once said the only sin in marketing is being boring. So take a stand. Be yourself. If you're outrageous and funny, let that flow. If you're unassuming and trustworthy, get that out there. Video gives you the opportunity to forge a very personal connection. And you can't do that if you're holding back on what makes you unique. Yes, you'll lose some folks. But the ones you connect with will stay for life.

Taking Your Video Viral

One of the most affordable (it's free!) and effective ways to materially increase your opt-in conversions is by taking your video viral—in other words, letting others help you spread the word to their friends, family members, associates, mailing lists, and so forth. Online marketing superstar Stephan Pierce explains how he turns viral YouTube videos into web traffic and paying customers.

Recently our company created a content-rich educational video called *A Clean Bill of Wealth* and uploaded it to YouTube (you can view it by searching for this title at www.YouTube.com). Because the video offered valuable information, within two days we have had 8,044 views, 33 comments, and it has been a favorite 38 times.

How does this lead to income? At the beginning and end of the video, it directs you to www.ACleanBillOfWealth.com, which leads to one of our products, the manual *Unleash Your Mind Power*. And because the product had a compelling offer, within two days we made over $1,000 selling a $47 e-book.

Here's a YouTube tip: When you put together your description for the video, type in your domain name at the end of the description. In order to make sure the link is active, use the full path http://www. (Don't just use something like www.yourname.com.) It will show up as an active hyperlink so when people click on the "More" link in the description, they'll be directed to your web site.

As I said earlier in this chapter, it is really important that your video is well done, inspirational and/or funny, entertaining, and memorable. Otherwise, no one—not even your mom—will send it to others! Following are some additional things you can do to ensure that your video gets passed along:

- **Keep it short.** There's no need for a mini series; in fact, the shorter, the better. Your first video should be less than two minutes.

- **Make sure it's clear and simple.** Don't make your viewers guess what you're trying to communicate.

- **Appeal to your viewers' emotions.** We all have enough information, no matter how powerful it is. So if you want your viewers to share your video with others, make them laugh or cry or tug at their heart strings. After all, who can resist a good belly laugh or a life-changing insight?

- **Ask your viewers to pass it on.** Don't assume your visitors know what to do; ask them to send your video to others. Also, ask your web designer to create a "tell a friend" area on the web page right below your video link.

- **Have a clear call to action.** If you want viewers to visit your web site, make sure you tell them how to get there!

Video Blogging

As I discussed in Chapter 4, blogs are wonderful alternatives, or additions to, more traditional web sites because of the following:

- they can be up and running quickly, usually in a matter of minutes
- anyone can use their professional-looking templates without any prior design and/or navigation experience or expertise
- they're inexpensive, dynamic, and fresh, and since new content is added regularly and often, the search engines love them.

Even better, using their technology and templates, you can now easily embed audio and video into your blog with the click of a mouse.

Video expert Rob Schultz has a terrific, free downloadable e-course designed to help you jump-start your own viral movies, whether you want to build buzz around a new product, boost attention for a seminar, or anything in between. Check out his web site at: www.ViralMovieMarketingSecrets.com.

PART 3: TELECONFERENCING AND WEB CONFERENCING

TELECONFERENCES AND TELESEMINARS SIMPLIFIED

Teleconferences—group phone meetings—have traditionally been used by large corporations and government agencies. However, as prices continue to plummet, small-business owners increasingly conduct meetings, training sessions, and the like, using this technology.

Similarly, teleseminars are group classes held over the phone, and, like teleconferences, entrepreneurs are using them more and more to help build better relationships with their prospects, create educational products for their customers, and deliver instructional material to their employees, among other things.

Teleseminars are extremely flexible. For instance, they can be your online product (e.g., a nine-week home redecorating course), internal training vehicle (e.g., direct sales instruction), or a marketing communications tool (e.g., an alternate vehicle for delivering your e-mail mini course). Teleconferences and teleseminars represent wonderful, cost-effective alternatives to in-person meetings and classes. Additionally, they are

- **Convenient**. They can be scheduled at the last minute and participants can call in from anywhere.

- **Efficient**. Important information can be delivered to groups of people effectively, affordably, and quickly.

- **Profitable**. You can sell your wisdom, knowledge, or advice by creating your own teleseminar,

OTHER WAYS THEY CAN HELP GROW AN ONLINE BUSINESS

While the list is endless, following are some additional ways teleconferences and teleseminars can work for you. Think of using one or the other to help you

- **Build your prospect lists.** Offer free teleseminars and use an opt-in box on your web site to gather prospect's e-mail addresses.

> **We cannot solve our problems** with the same level of thinking that created them."
>
> —*Albert Einstein, German physicist*

- **Gain credibility.** Creating and delivering relevant educational instruction on a given topic will help establish you as a subject matter expert—one of the first steps in gaining your prospects' trust.

- **Motivate and instruct others.** Conduct motivational, informational, brainstorming, and/or problem-solving teleconferences with your associates, affiliates, employees, sales force, and so on.

- **Deliver superior customer support.** Consider offering live Q-and-A sessions for new customers who need trouble-shooting advice, more detailed directions, updates, and the like.

- **Repurpose written content.** Record a teleseminar and transcribe the content into articles, e-books, workshops, etc.—and vice versa.

> ## "The workplace should primarily be
>
> an incubator for the human spirit."
>
> —*Anita Roddick, founder of The Body Shop*

- **Enhance your marketing communication.** For example, make a CD recording of your tele-class and include it in your media kit to showcase your interview skills or offer as a free incentive for prospects.

GETTING STARTED

After you've identified your target market and created relevant content, all you need is the following:

- **A service provider.** You'll need a teleconferencing service to host your call (i.e., provide the bridge line). Some are free; others charge a per-line or per-minute fee, or an ongoing subscription, or a flat rate.

- **A phone.** A land line is more reliable for clear and consistent audio reception and a must if you're the moderator. It's best to test this out ahead of time.

- **A headset.** While not a requirement, a high-quality, wired (not wireless) headset is great to have and your neck will be grateful.

For details on how to create and run successful teleseminars, go to www.Masteringteleseminars.com.

Now two quick cautions: Remember, not all web conferencing systems are equally functional on all computers. If any of your participants use Macs, make sure your provider's software is Mac friendly or find a service that is web supported. Also, make sure your provider has instructions for dealing with firewall barriers and that all participants are notified about them ahead of time.

WEB CONFERENCING AND WEBINARS SIMPLIFIED

Today's state-of-the-art internet technologies and software now make it effortless for groups of people to convene face-to-face anytime, any place. Web conferences are real-time, interactive audiovisual meetings held by phone and/or internet. Webinars are facilitator-led seminars using the same technology. Both allow online marketers to share documents, make presentations, demonstrate products and services, and so forth, using only a phone, a computer, and an internet connection. They provide a far more intimate experience than teleconferences because participants see and hear pictures, voices, and other attendees in real time. Also, like live conferences and seminars, these virtual reality vehicles provide on-the-spot interactivity between users who can do such things as ask and answer questions, conduct surveys, and take polls.

THE MAIN ADVANTAGES OF WEBINARS AND WEB CONFERENCING

In addition to being reliable substitutes for in-person meetings and/or seminars, they are:

- **Very affordable.** Now groups can meet for only a fraction of the costs associated with traveling to and from site locations.

- **More convenient and less time sensitive.** They can be scheduled more quickly and participants can attend wherever they are (as long as they have a phone, a computer, and/or internet access).

Go Toll Free

Nowadays, companies combine technologies to make it even easier for others to reach them. So another way to build credibility with prospects and customers, increase your mobility, and set up instant teleconferences is to place a toll-free number on your web site and use it in a whole new way. For instance, you can forward your toll-free calls to any phone, so you never have to worry about missing an important call. You can turn any call into a mini-teleconference by simply putting the first caller on hold and adding participants. If you'd like more information about these types of services, visit www.Accuconference.com.

- **Flexible.** Sessions can be recorded and archived for broadcasting anytime—over and over again—and/or turned into superior marketing content for your web site. Camtasia is excellent for computer recording. To find out more, visit www.techsmith.com.

They offer all of the advantages and opportunities of teleconferencing and teleseminars, while providing a far more intimate, lifelike environment because participants can see and hear in real time. Imagine live video bringing you the expressions, gestures, setting, and demonstrations of speakers and fellow participants. Imagine remote team collaborations, where visual illustrations, mind maps, and project plans are updated for all to see on the spot. That is the power of web-conferencing technology. Although web conferencing software service offerings vary, most will let you do the following:

- **Add video and audio.** Deliver live visuals of your presenters and participants; show a pre-recorded product or training demo; test your television commercial or YouTube promotion; and add music or sound effects to your webinar.

- **Create presentations and slideshows.** Deliver PowerPoint presentations and incorporate PDFs with live links.

- **Share files.** Allow groups to access shared files for project planning, team consensus, updating, product demonstrations, and so on.

- **Manage participant involvement.** Create live Q and A sessions, real-time polling, group chats, and more.

To see all of these features in action, go to www.EasyLiveConference.com.

Drawbacks and Limitations to Web Conferencing and Webinars

Although it improves each day, web conferencing technology is still evolving, which means that differences in equipment and connectivity can result in disconnects and other interesting session snafus. The best way to handle this is to warn attendees ahead of time and offer them instructions on what to do if they experience problems.

WHAT IS NEEDED TO CONDUCT WEB CONFERENCES AND/OR WEBINARS?

As with other internet multimedia vehicles, the entry costs are not prohibitive. You'll need:

- **Hardware.** In order to demonstrate and access documents in real time, you should have a high-quality computer capable of handling multimedia

Six Tips For Great Web Conferences

Teleconferencing and web conferencing are constantly improving, but there are still challenges. Here are a few simple tips to avoid some of the most common problems.

1. **Use land lines.** For excellent sound quality and fewer connection problems it's best to stick with a provider who uses land lines (phone company provided service). However, if your web-conference provider uses an internet phone service, such as VOIP (voice over internet protocol), make sure they use private internet cables as opposed to public.

2. **Test the help line.** Choose a provider that offers real time assistance. You and your participants will find it frustrating and annoying if you're put on hold for long periods of time or have to endure voice prompts before getting help from a live human being. Call a company's help line to check this out before signing up for their service.

3. **Surpass the software.** Look for a service that allows you manage your conference from a web site without having to download software—a far easier and more reliable option. And since these systems do not interfere with firewalls, more people will be free to participate.

4. **Take control.** We've all been in meetings where people veer off topic, talk over each other, or ambient noise makes it hard to hear. These problems can ruin a teleconference. Make sure your provider offers live call controls, which enable you to see who is present; select who is heard; disconnect uninvited visitors; and mute noisy lines. For added security, request single-use PINs. They prevent participants from distributing their access codes to uninvited listeners.

5. **Add graphics and other multimedia.** Research shows that the average conference lasts 15 percent longer when it includes graphics. Upgrading from the teleconference to the web conference increases participation and gets more involvement and higher-quality questions.

6. **Customize.** Custom options can make a big difference in the success of your conference or webinar. For example, you may want your provider to make reminder calls to your participants, hold a pre-conference session, review the agenda, and/or have instant playback capability. Make sure the service you choose has all of the options you will need.

— *Jim Black, expert in teleconferencing (easyliveconference.com)*

functions. If you want to upload your own audio and video, get an inexpensive camcorder and digital voice recorder.

■ **Software**. Cutting edge web conference services let you and your participants simply sign into a web environment without downloading any software. If you want to produce slide shows, all you need is presentation software, such as Microsoft PowerPoint. But if you want to add live audiovisuals and web links, and have remote access to your client's computer, you and your participants will need to download your service provider's conferencing software.

■ **Web conferencing service provider.** Web-conferencing service providers offer phone and web site support for your teleconference via a password-protected web environment and/or downloadable software. As with teleconferencing, you can rely on free services such as www.moodle.com or paid services such as Accuconference.com's Insight (web supported) and Meeting Central (software supported).

■ **Hands-free telephone.** It is best to use a landline and a headset.

WEB WORK: YOUR INTERACTIVE ADVENTURE

Now that you've learned the basics of online audio and video, it's your turn.

1. Visit a dozen or so sites online that use audio, and make notes on what you like or dislike about them. Here are a few to get you started: www. ezinequeen. com, www.audaciousaudio.com, and www.MitchSongs.com.

2. Here are two web audio creation services to check out: www. InstantFlashAudio.com and www.AudioAcrobat.com.

3. Visit a dozen or so sites online that use video, and make notes on what you like or dislike about them. Here are two to get you started: www. InternetVideoGuy.com and www.CarpetDepotDecatur.com.

4. Check out web video creation services, such as www.InstantFlashVideo. com and www.YouTube.com. Upload a video at www.YouTube. com.

5. If you want more information about teleconferencing, visit www.Free ConferenceCall.com, www.EasyLiveConference.com, or Google teleconferencing.

6. For audio or video conferencing, visit www.EasyLiveConference.com and register for a free demo, or Google "videoconferencing" to find others.

7. To explore or purchase audio tools (mikes, headphones, interfaces, or recording equipment) visit www.OnlineMarketingSuperstore.com.

CHAPTER 8 REMINDERS

Before moving on to Chapter 9, "Traffic Strategies: The Key to Getting More Visitors to Your Site," let's take a minute to review the most important lessons learned from this chapter:

- Multimedia—audio and video—can significantly reduce the time it takes to build relationships with prospects and customers.

- The type of multimedia you use depends on the type of web site you have and your product and service offerings.

- Today's affordable software and hardware make it easier than ever to integrate powerful multimedia into your e-commerce site, and ensure that your visitors can hear and view them on multiple devices such as iPods, MP3 players, laptops, and so on.

> ❝ **We are the creative force of our life,** and through our own decisions rather than our conditions, if we carefully learn to do certain things, we can accomplish those goals."
>
> —*Stephen Covey, author of* The Seven Habits of Highly Effective People

CHAPTER 9

TRAFFIC STRATEGIES

The Key to Getting More Visitors to Your Site

In this chapter you'll learn

- *what you need to know about search engine optimization*

- *the 12 best strategies for getting traffic to your web site*

- *how to track your web traffic*

...and much more.

> ## "Web traffic is a science.
>
> It is not magic; it is not a trick; it is not a secret. There are a set of fundamental laws and underlying principles that will govern why people visit a site and make a purchase online."
>
> —*Dearl Miller, internet traffic expert*
> *(www.OnlineTrafficNow.com)*

Think you're ready to start building your web site traffic? Before you spend time and money getting people to your site, make sure it's ready. Does it look professional? Is it user-friendly and easy to navigate? Is your sales letter well written? And most importantly, have you used the techniques I covered in Chapter 6 to convert your visitors once they arrive?

If so, congratulations! Now it's time to learn ways to get your targeted prospects—those folks who are actively looking for your products and/or services—to your web site. There are many ways to generate traffic; so many, in fact, that there are entire books on the subject and many internet experts who specialize in only one area of the topic. In this chapter, however, I focus on the techniques that my clients, other online marketing superstars, and I have found to be most effective, especially for beginners. The method or methods you choose will depend on many factors—your skills, time, product or service type, budget, interests, and so forth.

Additionally, I provide resources at the end of the chapter for those who are ready to try more advanced traffic tactics and/or would like more detailed information about these strategies or others.

For simplicity, I've broken the chapter down into two parts. The first is a primer on search engine optimization and the second is my list of the 12 best techniques for increasing your web site traffic.

PART 1: SEARCH ENGINE OPTIMIZATION 101

E-commerce web site owners have a unique advantage over more traditional retailers: online shoppers are actively looking for them, and that's not always the case for brick-and-mortar stores. With a bit of typing and a simple click of a mouse, millions of people all over the world go to search engines (e.g., Google, MSN, Yahoo!, AOL, AskJeeves, Dogpile, etc.) to hunt for specific products, services, information and/or opportunities. After typing in a word or phrase that describes what they're searching for, and pressing "Enter," they receive a results list that includes many direct links to appropriate web sites. And you guessed it: the closer your site appears to the top of the list, the better.

People who are searching naturally assume that the sites listed first—particularly those on the first page—are the best, and that's where they click. The concept may be uncomplicated but the methods for achieving these coveted positions—which are awarded to the search engines' favorite picks—are not. The good news is, however, that you don't have to become a techno junkie to raise your web site's position over time. Rather, you need to understand and apply consistently simple, but powerful, strategies—then be prepared to wait. And since the vast majority of online sales begin with search engines, they are an extremely valuable resource for any e-commerce business.

But before I get too far, I'd like to step back a bit to present some search engine basics—a high-level overview of key concepts that will add clarity and perspective, especially if you're a beginner.

WHAT ARE SEARCH ENGINES AND WHAT MAKES THEM SO IMPORTANT?

Search engines are really nothing more than electronic internet services that allow their users to search the world wide web or other databases for information links to web sites. Although there are many, the most powerful (called the Big Three) are Google (www.Google.com), Yahoo! (www.Yahoo.com) and MSN (www.Msn.com).

Their two main objectives are to earn profitable revenues by selling internet advertising space to businesses around the world, and to maintain and grow their user base by providing visitors with the most relevant and highest-quality links and resource results. It's important to note that the second goal supports the first. That is, the search engines don't make money unless they attract advertisers. And they can't attract advertisers without an audience. Therefore, the more people like a given search engine, the more likely they are to visit it, over and over again.

HOW DO SEARCH ENGINES ENSURE THEY DELIVER SUPERIOR RESULTS?

Simply put, they check out millions of internet pages everyday. Here's how: Search engines send out electronic *spiders* (also called *crawlers* and *bots*) that act as their foot soldiers. (Don't worry, they're not as ominous as they sound).

These constantly and regularly crawl new and updated web site pages (not whole sites) and collect information. Then they bring the data back to their respective search engines where it is sorted and stored, or indexed.

Whenever they receive a request, the search engines apply their own set of mathematical rules, called algorithms (which are secret and continually altered) to find and extract the most appropriate content from their cached database. Then they place the link to the information on their results list—all in a blink of an eye.

I'd like to reiterate a significant point in case you missed it: Search engines do not perform live internet queries; they grab their information from the data contained in their indices. This is important to understand because search engine spiders check most web pages once or twice a month (even though some get crawled more often), which explains why it takes a while for new pages to appear in results lists. More importantly, it also means that when a new web site first becomes live on the internet, the search engines don't know it exists, therefore won't be included in their results lists until they find it.

Bottom line: You can't just put up your web site and expect the search engines to begin sending you qualified prospects right away. It's not an overnight process!

There are however, things you can do while your site is being built (and after) to improve your standings with the search engines. The process is called *search engine optimization* or *SEO*. It includes, at a high level, on-page factors (things that you do to the pages on your web site) and off-page factors (things that you do externally to your web site pages). As you'll see, there are several requisite items—things you must do upfront—and a number of items you'll work on over time. If you're going to do well with the search engines it's important that you remember the following four things:

1. **Patience is a virtue.** Slow and steady wins the race; it may take weeks or even months before some engines locate your site.

2. **Search engines cannot be fooled.** You can't trick them into giving you a high or top position for your main keywords. All of the major (and secondary) search engines use stringent security measures specifically designed to prevent trickery.

3. **There is no one huge thing you can do right away.** No single tactic will materially improve your chances of moving up quickly with the search engines. There are a number of little things that, when combined, can have a dramatic effect on your ranking (depending upon your niche and your competition).

4. **Do not overfocus on SEO.** Learn and apply the basics and forget the rest. If you concentrate on building meaningful relationships; offering valuable products, services, and great information; and applying the strategies in this chapter; the rest will fall in line.

WAYS TO OPTIMIZE YOUR WEB SITE

Keywords and Phrases

Keywords are those elusive but vitally important words and phrases that internet users type into search fields when they're hunting for just about anything. Your keywords are the building blocks of all of your marketing efforts and they contain the power to make, or break, your ability to get the right traffic to your e-commerce site. That's why you must be willing to spend the time and effort necessary to make sure they contain an accurate description of your product and service and are commonly used by your target audience.

In order for search engines to find you (and deem you relevant) you'll need to include your most powerful keywords in various places on your web site—your copy, headings, anchor and footer text, and alongside photos and graphics. But don't overdo; if

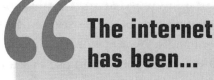

The internet has been...

the most fundamental change during my lifetime and for hundreds of years. Someone the other day said, It's the biggest thing since Gutenberg, and then someone else said No, it's the biggest thing since the invention of writing."

—*Rupert Murdoch, media mogul*

you've been using the internet for a while you probably remember landing on web pages that contained words or phrases that were used over and over again, even when they didn't make sense! Years ago many online marketers used this tactic to increase their *keyword density*—the percentage of specific keywords versus all other words on the page. Why? Because in those days search engines equated higher keyword density with increased relevance, which meant that pages containing the most were bumped closer to the top of the results list. This, of course, translated into more traffic!

This is not the case today. Overloading your site's pages with keywords will not help you and if the search engines suspect that you're stuffing your pages inappropriately, it will actually hurt you. While it's important to use keywords frequently and appropriately throughout your site, I suggest that you limit your keywords to *no more than a 3 to 5 percent* density ratio. You can double-check your keyword density for free on www.KeywordDensity.com. Additionally, you should use no more than one or two different keywords or key phrases on any given page

> ## "Opportunities multiply as they are seized."
>
> —*Sun Tzu, author of* The Art of War

and save your most important ones for your home page. Here are some other quick tips for using keywords effectively:

- **Use a keyword search tool** to help you discover which ones your targeted prospects use most often. Some good ones are www.Wordtracker.com and www.KeywordDiscovery.com. Begin by choosing keywords or phrases that you would use to search for your products or services and let the tools help you from there.

- **Check out your competitors.** Visit their sites and read their pages carefully to discover what keywords and phrases they're using.

- **Use related search options.** These are available through the major search engines as well as smaller ones such as www.Gigablast.com and www.Vivisimo.com.

- **Place your keywords in paragraphs, headings, and bulleted lists.** In other words, put them in the visible text on your page.

- **Position your keywords up front in your page copy.** Early and often is a good rule of thumb, but don't stuff your page copy with keywords.

■ **Incorporate your keywords into your internal and external links.** Or surround them with your keywords.

■ **Run your own searches.** Use singular and plural versions of keywords to find out if the results are different. If so, use both forms in your copy.

■ **Use your keywords or phrases in your domain name.** If you've already got your domain name selected, you can use your keywords in your page names; for example, www. yourdomain. com/ yourkeyword.htm.

■ **Avoid keywords or phrases that are too generic.** Remember, the more your keywords describe exactly what you do, the better.

■ **Don't target individual words.** Multi-keyword phrases will help you get more targeted traffic.

■ **Mix up your keywords.** For example, if your words are "gold wedding bands," try "gold bands" and "wedding bands" also.

On-Page Factors: Title, Meta Tags, and Visible Copy

People scour the internet looking for information and search engines deliver the links to that information, but they don't read it the same way. People judge content by reading words and listening to sounds. Search engines, however, read HTML code (which is translated into the words, colors, and designs that we see). The

Million Dollar Tip

Online marketing superstar Jon Keel (www.improved-results.com), who has helped businesses worldwide with his performance traffic strategies, offers the following suggestions for finding out exactly what keywords your competitors think are important:

Step 1: Type in your competitor's URL.

Step 2: In the web browser (Explorer or Foxfire) window, click on View.

Step 3: In the drop-down window, click on either Source or Page Source.

Step 4: What appears next in a new window is the actual HTML code for your competitor's web page. Now, at the top of the page look for the following between the <head> and </head> tags:

<title>   This is the title tag.
What keywords is your competitor using?

<meta description> This is the meta description tag.
Are there any keywords listed here?

<meta keywords>   This is the meta keywords tag.
Are there any keywords listed here?

most important place on the page to include keywords is in the *title tag,* the wording you see in the blue bar at the extreme top of your browser window. The title tag should be different for every page on your site since each page should be focused around a different priority keyword.

Meta tags provide additional ways to use your keywords in non-visible content that can help you obtain a higher position in the results lists. *Meta description tags* and *meta keyword tags* are the only two on which you should focus. Depending upon the search engine, the meta description tag might be the narrative shown for your web site. Here are some tips for getting general and page title meta tags right:

- **Use unique page titles and meta tags,** and focus on your most important keywords one at a time.

- **Limit meta descriptions to a few sentences** and no more than a paragraph.

- **Use real-people words** when developing your page and title tags. In most cases, people don't care about your company name.

- **Include common misspellings, abbreviations, acronyms, and synonyms in your tags.**

- **Use keywords to help improve the look and clarity of your page.** For instance, use them in your headlines, subheads, and other central dividing areas on the page. This makes it easier for people and search engines to see them.

- **Don't use overly generic tags.** "Teaching parakeets to talk" is good, "birds" is not.

- **Avoid tag pages or titles with salutations.** For example, "welcome page" and "home page" say nothing about your content and reduce your keyword density.

Use Search-Friendly Design and Navigation Techniques

As I discussed in detail in Chapter 4, your e-commerce site should appeal to your visitors. Among other things, it must be professional and pleasant looking, well written, and easy to use. However, here are some additional design and navigation tips that you can use to ensure that you'll please the search engines.

- Use text in your navigation links and use alt text with images. Search engine spiders don't read graphics, so using alt tags solves this problem.

- Use CSSs (cascading style sheets) to enhance your pages' appearance and to prevent HTML tags from appearing too large.

- Include a site map; your visitors will appreciate it and search engine spiders will be able to crawl your site more quickly.

Internal Web Page Links

You'll want to make sure it is easy for search engines (and more importantly, your visitors) to find their way from one of your web pages to any other via internal links. Here are some tips for setting up effective internal links:

- Provide a link to your home page from every other page on your site.

- Include links from your home page to all major pages (e.g., FAQs, Products, Services, Order Now) and links to all primary pages from every page on your site.

- If possible, describe your links. For instance, "Frequently Asked Questions" is better than "Click Here." If that's not possible, use footers (text links found at the bottom of the page) to explain more about your links.

- Regularly check your site for broken links. This is particularly important if you're going to submit your site to directories.

- Provide regular and multiple links to other pages from long pages. For example, allow your visitors to quickly move to other web pages without having to scroll to the very beginning or end of the page they're currently viewing.

Add Valuable and Relevant Content

As I said earlier, search engines decode keywords in an attempt to provide their users with pertinent and appropriate *content* links. So, in addition to choosing the most relevant keywords you'll also want to make sure that you overdeliver valuable content; your prospects will love you for it, and so will the search engines! What do I mean by valuable content? Simply said, it can be any information that is related to your products and/or services; useful and applicable; objective (not a sales pitch); and the like. It's your chance to help your customers and prospects stay informed on your industry, trends, current events, breakthroughs, and innovations. Examples include special reports, articles (written by you or others), e-mail newsletters (e-zines), mini classes, columns, audio files, free software, public domain documents (see, for example, www.commoncontent.org and www.gnu.org/copyleft), and blogs, just to name a few. Just make sure they're meaty, well written, entertaining, and compelling!

Following are some quick tips for adding great information to your site:

- **Add and update your content regularly.** Don't do it all at once; otherwise, you'll discourage the search engines from making repeat visits.

- **Make it interactive.** Showcase your visitors' feedback and comments and allow others to join in.

- **Don't go it alone.** Use other experts' advice as well, but be sure to ask permission, acknowledge the source and link to their sites.

- **Incorporate RSS feeds.** They allow for automatic updating of content-rich documents.

- **Link to local, state, and federal government sites.** This is a very easy and extremely helpful way to add instant content.

Submit your Site to Directories

It is a good idea to submit new sites and updated web pages to internet directories, where real humans actually compile and categorize web site lists! There are hundreds of directories—general, specific, big, and small. The bigger ones usually charge a recurring yearly fee (e.g., http://dir.yahoo.com and http://directory.google.com) while smaller ones will either charge a one-time fee or none at all. Most directories do not charge for listing non-commercial sites and offer free regional listings to e-commerce sites.

One of the most popular free-listing syndicated directories is the Open Directory Project at www.dmoz.com. It's worth considering, even though you'll have to wait for one of the editors to check out your site. Also, no matter which directory you choose, make sure you follow its sign-up directions carefully.

Here are some quick tips for choosing directories:

> ## It doesn't matter how many times you fail.
>
> It doesn't matter how many times you almost get it right. No one is going to know or care about your failures, and neither should you. All you have to do is learn from them and those around you because... All that matters in business is that you get it right once. Then everyone can tell you how lucky you are."
>
> —*Mark Cuban, American entrepreneur and owner of the Dallas Mavericks*

- Submit your site to directories that are reputable, well known in your industry and interesting. Check out their Google PageRank™; it will give you a good indication of their importance.

- Start submitting to smaller directories. They may have a smaller audience, but they're often more targeted, which will result in more traffic. Plus you'll only have to pay a one-time fee.

- Don't overthink this process. Submit your site to logical directories and then move on.

- Avoid directories that require you to link back to them. Directories are supposed to be listing your site, not plugging their own.

PART 2: STRATEGIES FOR INCREASING TRAFFIC

Now that you have a better, albeit very basic, understanding of ways to optimize your site for search engines, it's time to go one step further. In this section, I'll teach you the 12 most valuable strategies—at least in my experience—for increasing web site traffic. Please keep in mind that there are many, many more, which I simply cannot cover adequately without ending up with a 60-page chapter. So, I've purposely included the ones that I believe are most effective and actionable and least complicated. For more information on web traffic strategies, visit www.MasteringOnlineMarketing.com.

STRATEGY 1: SET UP AN E-MAIL SIGNATURE

Let's begin with a strategy that is so easy that you can do it in the next five minutes. Programming an automatic e-mail signature (or sig file)—putting your name, contact information, and/or an active link to your web site at the end of every e-mail—is simple, free, and extremely effective for increasing web site traffic.

Your e-mail program (e.g., Microsoft Outlook) will allow you to add a signature in minutes by following the directions usually located under its "Tools" tab. If you use Mac Mail, look in the "System Preferences" folder. Following are some quick tips for setting up your e-mail signature:

■ Make your signature clear, and include your top keywords and an active link to your web site. For example:

Want to fly Navy jets?
Learn how at: www.NavyGuides.com

Potty Train Your Toddler in 24 Hours
www.AskThePottyTrainer.com

■ Think with a marketing mindset. Your goal is to offer a compelling benefit that interests the reader enough to click through. For example,

Mitch Meyerson, author, speaker, and consultant
Get Free Traffic-Building Tips with the #1 Multi-media Mini Course on the Web
www.MitchMeyerson.com

■ Look at your colleagues' and competitors' signatures. It's not necessary to reinvent the wheel; learn from others.

■ Consider adding a graphic to your signature file. Try something small but attention grabbing (however, sometimes this can increase the chances that your e-mail will get blocked by your receiver's spam filter).

STRATEGY 2: USE A VARIETY OF LINKS

One of the biggest mistakes online marketers commit is thinking they can grow and maintain a thriving online business by themselves. It simply can't be done without other people. Think of the internet as one huge community that affords us the opportunity to exchange ideas, meet new people, obtain valuable information, and find exceptional products and services. And while some view the internet as impersonal, I believe otherwise. When used correctly, it is the single most powerful tool available for improving the quality and increasing the quantity of healthy and lasting connections with like-minded people and groups, those who will become your and your online business' greatest supporters.

And *linking* with others is one of the best tools for making this happen. It will enable you to spread the news of your products and services faster, please your visitors and search engines, and increase targeted traffic. There are two types of links: inbound and outbound.

Inbound Links

Inbound links (also called backlinks) are direct one-way hyperlinks from another web site into yours. And because they act as a kind of objective vote for your web site, they are one of the best tools for improving your page ranking and results list position. However, they can also be the most difficult to obtain because there's little in it for the web owner who links one way into your site. Here are a couple of quick tips for getting good inbound links:

- Check out links into your site and your competitors' sites. Find out which, and how many, web sites link into them. For example, if one of your competitors' web sites is www.abcdefghi.com, here's an easy way to uncover the information: log on to Google (www.google.com) and type in "link:www.abcdefghi.com" and hit "Search." You'll get a list of web sites that link to your competitors. Contact the sites' owners and ask if they'll link with you; chances are, they will.

- Give something away. This technique will please your visitors and make your site more worthy of backlinks.

Outbound Links

Outbound links are the exact opposite of inbound links; in other words, they are one-way links from your site to others. Even though outbound links have no direct effect on how the major search engines rate your site, they will enhance your credibility with your visitors. Following are some quick tips for choosing the right outbound links:

- **Be choosy.** Linking with less than reputable sites can negatively affect your search engine ratings.

- **Pick sites that enhance your target audience's experience.** Find great resources, blogs, new sites, directories, portals, and so on that offer relevant and useful information.

- **Check out your competitors.** Find out where their outbound links terminate and visit those sites.

- **Avoid lumping the links all together.** Place them in logical spots throughout your web site.

STRATEGY 3: WRITE AND POST ARTICLES

Remember, the number one thing that people look for on the internet is information—news, products, and services, resources, technology, and much more—and what better place to find it? That's why writing and posting informative articles will increase your web site traffic and please the search engines. It's one of the easiest and most effective tools you can use; that is, unless you hate to write and/or have poor writing skills. If so, you should still consider hiring a freelance ghostwriter to pen some articles for you.

Following are some quick tips for writing and submitting online articles:

- **Write a meaty article on a subject related to your site.** Use your keywords and phrases throughout, offer solutions, and provide useful tips.

- **Use a resource box located at the end of the article.** Introduce yourself and include a direct link to your site and opt-in invitation. Make sure to have a clear and compelling call to action, like in your e-mail signatures.

- **Submit your article to one or more online sites.** Make sure to submit your writing to sites that make sense for your industry. Check out www.buzzle.com, www.IdeaMarketers.com, www.SubmitYourArticle.com, or www.ArticleCentral.com.

The Power of Article Submission

As Certified Guerrilla Marketing Coaches, we talk to business owners every day who are struggling to drive traffic to their web sites by paying out the wazoo for pay-per-click or expensive online advertising that quite often doesn't work. What we have found is that while these strategies can be effective, they are not necessarily the golden egg. Hear us loudly and clearly: You don't have to spend gobs of money to get traffic to your web site. Over the last decade, I have discovered how powerful online article submission can be. It can literally drive thousands of prospects to your web site while building credibility with your target market.

Following are eight steps for getting it right:

Step 1: **Choose a compelling topic.** Pick something interesting and relevant in today's world. Some of today's hottest internet article topics include business and marketing, finances and investments, health and wellness, home decorating, leadership, personal development/self improvement, pets, travel, writing.

Step 2: **Keep it short.** Your articles should be no longer than 500-700 words in length.

Step 3: **Choose your format.** Decide beforehand what type of article you'll write, such as a non-fiction narrative, story, interview, or how-to.

Step 4: **Create a rough draft for your article.** Begin with a list of what you know about the subject matter and let it flow from there.

Step 5: **Write the most important points in five short paragraphs.** If it's more than that, consider splitting it into Part I, Part II, and so on.

Step 6: **Write a powerful introduction.** Spell out the benefits the reader will gain by reading your article.

Step 7: **Write a powerful close.** Recap what they've learned and remind them of the main points.

Step 8: **Write the resource box** ("About the Author" paragraph). This is your opportunity to let the public know about you, your web site, and any other information that will enhance your credibility. Make sure to include a link back to your web site.

—*Bea Fields, president of www.FiveStarLeader.com*

- **Avoid sales pitches.** Don't tout whatever it is you're selling on your site. Instead, provide valuable information that will make the reader want to visit your site to learn more.

- **Do not copy or plagiarize content** that you find elsewhere on the internet. Enough said!

STRATEGY 4: PARTICIPATE IN DISCUSSIONS AND FORUMS

As I said earlier in this chapter, you should think of the internet as one big community of interests and people. Therefore one of your goals should be to connect with others who share your interests and are actively seeking your products and/or services. That's why participating in online conversations is an interesting, successful, and free method for bringing targeted traffic to your web site. Your biggest challenge lies in finding groups that are a good fit, but you can simplify the process by conducting online searches using keywords like discussion groups, forums, discussion boards, and the like. Once you've located a few appropriate forums, begin adding thoughtful comments, questions, and advice on topics that interest you.

> # Watch, listen, and learn.
>
> You can't know it all yourself…. Anyone who thinks they do is destined for mediocrity."
>
> —*Donald Trump, American businessman and entrepreneur*

Following are some quick tips for locating and participating in discussion groups:

- Post relevant and interesting content, and make sure it's really helpful to the group.

- Position yourself as an industry specialist (if you are).

- Include your signature file to make it easier for people to find you.

- Don't advertise—it's not allowed and you'll risk being banned from further participation.

STRATEGY 5:
WRITE AN E-ZINE

One of the most effective strategies for getting repeat traffic to your web site is to write and send consistent e-zines (e-mail newsletters). Remember, your mailing list can be a gold mine, but it won't be unless you use it to correspond regularly with your subscribers. You should create and implement a solid plan for delivering high-value content combined with compelling promotional offers.

STRATEGY 6:
USE PAY-PER-CLICK AND
ADWORD'S CAMPAIGNS

One of the most popular traffic-generating strategies on the internet is Google's (AdWords) and other search engines' pay-per-click campaigns. Simply put, web site owners place ads that appear on the results page (they're usually found from top to bottom on the far right-hand side of the page) and pay the search engine an agreed-upon amount every time an online visitor clicks through to their site.

The order in which your ad appears on that page is dependent

Tips from the E-Zine Queen

Alexandria K. Brown, the E-zine Queen, is an extremely successful marketing coach who authors a thriving e-zine. Here are her tips on publishing e-zines that get read (and make money):

1. **Be regular**—at least every two weeks, preferably once a week. If you reach out and touch clients and prospects less than that, your sales will suffer greatly.

2. **Keep it short**—articles are fine, just keep them short enough to read on the spot. I recommend around 500 words. Other ideas include Q and As, top ten lists, and quick tips.

3. **Publish in HTML**—this means your e-mails have color and graphics. Studies prove HTML e-mails get higher readership and higher response. Just keep it simple.

4. **Be personal**—write your e-zine from a person, not a company. People buy from people, and from people they know, like, and trust. So write like a friend would write.

5. **Make it useful**—remember that your readers subscribed to get helpful information. Give 'em what they want and don't just blab on and on about you and your company.

6. **Toot your horn**—as long as you stick to #5, you can also promote the heck out of yourself and your business! So go for it—use at least 25 percent of your e-mail message for this.

7. **Call 'em to action**—end each issue with a clear and concise offer, whether it's for a free consultation, a discount on your products, or a click here to learn more about X.

You can get a copy of Alexandria's free report "The 3 Simple Secrets to Publishing an Ezine That Makes You Money" at www.EzineQueen.com.

on many factors, primarily the amount you're willing to pay for certain keywords or phrases, relative to others.

It's simple to set up a pay-per-click campaign—just go to each search engine's main page and click on "Advertising Programs" and follow the links and instructions from there. (Google has some of the best videos on the web; the ones for AdWords are located at www.google.com/adwords/learningcenter/index.html.)

However, it's a whole other story when it comes to effectively managing a campaign, and you can go broke fast if you don't know what you're doing and/or are not willing to monitor it very, very carefully. That's why I usually suggest that online marketing novices pass on pay-per-click advertising until they've had more experience. Why is it so difficult? Because there are way too many variables to consider, some which can have a significant effect on the prices you'll pay per keyword or phrase.

Here are just a few of the things that can change your results dramatically:

■ **How well your 120-character ad is worded.** If it's too general, you may get traffic but you will probably end up paying for visitors who aren't likely to become customers.

■ **Negative keywords.** The keywords you use are important, but you also have to think about the words you want excluded from the search results.

■ **Your daily budget.** If your keyword cost is high and your budget is low, your ad will be shown intermittently throughout the day.

■ **Your click-through rate.** Google will often reward you and place you higher up on the list if your percentage of click-throughs is higher than your competitors'.

And the list goes on. The best advice I can give you is before you consider setting up a pay-per-click campaign, study it carefully and create a well-thought-out plan. If you want to learn all of the ins and outs of pay-per-clicks, there's no one better to consult than Perry Marshall, AdWords expert and author of *The Ultimate Guide to Google AdWords.* To see a special Google AdWords Cheat Sheet he created, visit www.MasteringOnlineMarketing/PerryMarshall.htm.

Once you get more comfortable with your keywords, you may want to consider setting up an AdWords campaign and use it exclusively to test which keywords are converting best. The great thing about this is you'll get vital information in a matter of hours or days!

STRATEGY 7: WRITE ONLINE PRESS RELEASES

Great advertising looks nothing like advertising; that's why so many smart online entrepreneurs take advantage of free and/or low-cost and highly effective traffic-generating strategies such as online press releases (PRs). There are a number of free resources on the internet offering guidance on using press releases to not only generate traffic to your web site but also obtain inbound links. Do a search on Google or any of the other big search engines for "online press release" or "free press release info."

In addition to their direct benefits, online press releases can further establish you as a trusted expert in your field; help you reach a worldwide audience in minutes, and afford a number of different ways for delivering your message (e.g., using pdf documents, podcasting, etc.) Here are some quick tips for improving you online PR efforts:

- **Combine online and offline strategies for maximum effectiveness.** It's a good idea to use a combination of methods to garner attention, so mix offline channels such as newspapers, TV, and radio with your online efforts.

- **Tie yourself, your company, and/or your products and services to a regional or national news story.**

- **Use press release services.** Services such as www.PRweb.com have various contribution levels depending upon the amount of exposure and additional tools you'll want to use.

- **Make sure your press release is clear and well written.** Edit, edit, and edit some more. Remember, the nichier the better, and don't be too salesy—remember, it's not about you!

- **Use press releases frequently.** They are not one-shot deals.

- **Prepare answers to questions ahead of time.** Don't be taken off guard.

- **Don't stick to convention.** Controversy is okay as long as it's done tastefully. So stick your neck out, stand up for something, and shout it to the world.

STRATEGY 8: SET UP A REFERRAL PROGRAM USING TELL-A-FRIEND SCRIPTS

Word-of-mouth referrals are the best advertising money can't buy. Why? Because, according to a recent study conducted by eMarketer.com, approximately 53 percent of online traffic came from recommendations made by family members and/or friends during the previous 30 days. So, why not save your visitors a phone call and make it simple and convenient for them to suggest your site to others? Here's how:

- **Get a tell-a friend script online.** It doesn't have to be long or involved (and many shopping carts offer them for free) and you can find lots of ideas online. (Google "tell a friend forms.")

- **Offer a compelling incentive.** For example, give free merchandise to your visitors (and their referees) for providing the names and e-mail addresses of friends and relatives who may be interested in your site.

- **Place your tell-a-friend form on a free download page.** There's no better time to ask for a referral or link. A good example can be found at www.GMarketingFreebies.com.

- **Add a tell-a-friend script to your e-zines.** Your e-zine recipients are your loyal readers, so ask them to spread the word!

STRATEGY 9: COMBINE ONLINE AND OFFLINE STRATEGIES

As well as online traffic generators, take advantage of every opportunity to advertise your web site offline, by including information about it on everything, such as:

- **your business stationery: cards, letterhead, checks, invoices**

- **specialty ad gifts: pens, T-shirts, hats, water bottles**

- **seminars:** this is a perfect time to say "For your free seven-part special report go to www.mydomain.com."

- **voice-mail greetings:** record messages such as "Visit my web site at…"

- **ads:** newspaper, radio, TV, yellow pages, billboards, brochures, leaflets
- **columns and articles** for your local magazine or newspaper (include your URL at the bottom)

Mention your site anytime you are talking about your business. Don't be intrusive; just find the right moment to let people know it exists and why they should go there. For 100 more marketing strategies, visit www.gmarketing-coach.com/weapons.htm.

STRATEGY 10: PARTICIPATE IN AFFILIATE PROGRAMS

An affiliate program is a system for recruiting, supporting, and rewarding other people for selling products. You may participate as an *affiliate* (someone who sells other people's products) or *affiliate program owner* (someone who recruits other people to sell his or her products). If you have good products and/or services and a strong sales page, I strongly advise you to consider setting up your own affiliate program. It's one of the best ways to get traffic to your site (i.e., others will be more than happy to send you prospects). However, I discuss both types of affiliate programs in greater detail in Chapter 10.

STRATEGY 11: ADD ADDITIONAL CONTENT TO YOUR WEB SITE

In Strategy 3, I recommended writing and submitting articles to online publications. In many cases, the same articles (modified somewhat so they are not what the search engines term *duplicate content)* can be modified and added to your web site (perhaps in a special section called "Articles").

Why is this important? For several reasons. First, the search engine spiders will recognize that your site is ever changing—not static—and that you're committed to adding and updating relevant and valuable information for your visitors.

Second, as you continue to add content to your site, you'll find that visitors will type in an almost unlimited number of keywords to find you. If you know the keywords they use (which you can find in your web site's logs or stats software), you can add information that corresponds specifically to them.

Last, you want your site to be recognized as the authority or source of information for your niche. This in itself will give you an advantage with the search engines. It probably makes sense that, all other things being equal, a site with 50 pages of content is not as much of an authority on a given subject as a site with 500 pages of content.

STRATEGY 12: FORM JOINT VENTURE PARTNERSHIPS

Although I discuss this topic in great detail in Chapter 10, I think it's important to mention here that partnering with other online marketers is one of the most powerful tactics you can use to increase your web site's traffic. For example, I recently set up a special teleseminar interview with Michael Gerber, author of the best-selling book, *The E-Myth*. I knew my own list of subscribers would benefit from his sage advice and insights, so I was understandably thrilled when he agreed to join me.

> **If you don't have daily objectives,** you qualify as a dreamer."
>
> —*Zig Ziglar, American author and motivational speaker*

However, instead of inviting my subscribers only, I asked my colleague Melanie Benson Strick, a Gerber fan and successful online coach with a large mailing list of her own to co-host the seminar with me. I felt that her subscribers would be interested in participating as well, and Melanie agreed.

As a result, we co-promoted the event and after only one e-mail notification had more than 700 people opt in to the call, not to mention loads of traffic to our sites from the links on the sign-up page. This of course created more traffic than either one of us would have done alone. This is just one example of the many types of joint promotions available on the internet. I strongly suggest you seek out new partnerships to increase your exposure and traffic.

WEB WORK: YOUR INTERACTIVE ADVENTURE

1. Visit www.OnlineTrafficNow.com to get a free two-month membership to Trafficology, the best traffic membership site on the web. Its traffic-generating ideas and resources are invaluable.

2. Set up three e-mail signatures in your e-mail program (e.g., Outlook). Make sure you have an active link to your web site and a clear call to action (if needed, review this chapter for examples).

> ## "Genius is
> ## 1 percent inspiration
>
> and 99 percent perspiration. Accordingly a genius is often merely a talented person who has done all of his or her homework."
>
> —*Thomas Edison, American inventor*

3. Write a 500-word article in the area of your expertise including a resource box containing your brief bio and an active link to your web site. Then post the article to one of the directories suggested in this chapter.

4. Initiate link exchanges with a minimum of ten web site owners. Make sure their sites offer a compatible product or service for your visitors.

5. Find a few groups and/or forums that discuss topics that relate to your product or service. Post helpful comments and answer questions to position yourself as an expert in the field. Then add a link to your site. Do not pitch or sell.

6. Review the material on search engine optimization in this chapter and make the under-the-hood changes suggested in that section. If you are unclear on how to do this, contact a specialist in SEO.

7. Building a strong traffic-generating system requires an assortment of tactics that all work together. Choose at least ten from this chapter and monitor them using your traffic calendar. Use the template I've provided in Figure 9-1 (or get a downloadable version at www.Mastering OnlineMarketing.com) to make sure you stay on track.

FIGURE 9-1. Web Traffic Calendar		
STRATEGY	**NOTES**	**DATES AND COMPLETION**
1. SEO		
2. E-mail Signature		
3. Writing Articles		
4. Linking		
5. Posting in Discussion Forums		
6. Thank You and Order Pages		
7. Pay-Per-Click Campaigns		
8. Online Press Releases		
9. Tell-A-Friend Scripts		
10. Offline Strategies		
11.		
12.		
13.		

CHAPTER 9 REMINDERS

Before moving on to Chapter 10, "People Power: The Key to Successful Affiliate Programs and Partnerships," let's take a minute to review the most important lessons learned from this chapter:

■ To have a successful traffic-generation plan you must take a look under the hood and make sure you have all your tags, keywords, and coding done correctly. You must optimize this invisible area of your site so that search engines will find you.

■ Links are a very important aspect of traffic creation. Make sure you are linking to and from other relevant sites and that your internal links have keyword-rich alt tags.

■ Building traffic takes patience and consistent action on your plan.

■ Use a traffic calendar to track your efforts and adjust accordingly.

> **"People with clear, written goals**
> accomplish far more in a shorter period of time than people without them could ever imagine."
>
> —*Brian Tracy, motivational coach and author*

PEOPLE POWER

The Key To Successful Affiliate Programs and Partnerships

In this chapter you'll learn

- *how to form joint ventures and strategic alliances*

- *how to make money with affiliate programs*

- *how to create your own affiliate programs*

- *how to combine all of these tools for long-term wealth*

...and much more.

Talent wins games,

but teamwork and intelligence win championships."

—*Michael Jordan,
retired professional basketball player*

Contrary to popular belief, the widely successful lone ranger e-commerce entrepreneur rarely exists anymore. The internet is far too competitive for anyone to go it alone. Simply put, you need to help, and be helped by others. And while this may seem discouraging, it's really good news because teaming up with the right people can save you time, money, and stress; increase your reach and effectiveness; and make for far more enjoyable workdays.

Additionally, online marketers are pioneering a brave new business model—one that flies in the face of the former winner-takes-all, corporate form. Today's fresh internet culture encourages openness rather than propriety, cooperation instead of competition, and relationship building over bean counting. One of the most powerful benefits of this model—made easier because of existing and evolving state-of-the-art technologies—is that people now have the ability to team up with anyone on the planet! Gone are the days when entrepreneurs had to rely on a handful of local product and service providers—bookkeepers, database developers, consultants, and so on—to help them with vital business functions on a strictly cash-for-hire or commission basis. Today even the smallest businesses have the ability to join forces with others who can help them grow and sustain their businesses with one click of a mouse.

Even better, technology affords them the opportunity to prescreen their partnership choices discreetly by doing things like attending their teleseminars, downloading their free offers, viewing their web traffic rankings on Alexa (www.alexa.com), and joining their mailing lists.

In this chapter I discuss three of the most popular types of e-commerce partnerships: *joint ventures, strategic alliances,* and *affiliate programs.*

PART 1: THE POWER OF PARTNERSHIPS

When two people join forces—that is, work together on a common short- or long-term goal, project, or business—it allows each person to benefit emotionally, financially, and/or intellectually from the skills, knowledge, and resources that the other partner contributes. And for online marketers, these advantages may include increased mailing list size, ready access to industry experts, more compelling web site content, connections with powerful players, direct sales of products or services, and much more.

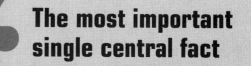

The most important single central fact

about a free market is that no exchange takes place unless both parties benefit."

—*Milton Friedman, American economist*

You'll also find that teaming up with talented people can geometrically explode both partners' creative potential. Here's how it worked for me: In 2004, I partnered with Michael Port, a talented businessman who conducted teleseminars aimed at helping entrepreneurs think bigger about their lives and businesses. We formed a mastermind group with four other innovators in the industry, in order to discuss current trends in the coaching and consulting fields. After many conversations, we were convinced that there was a growing, and unfilled, need in the marketplace for trustworthy professional advice on two very specific topics:

- how to create and market information products online
- how to increase targeted web site traffic

As a result, we created our first program, the Product Factory, a teleseminar that guides online marketers through all the steps involved in developing and marketing their own information products. After that, we created a second class, Online Traffic School, that helps people learn more effective ways to drive traffic to their web sites.

Michael and I continue to enjoy our working relationship and now regularly have more than 100 students enrolled in each program. You can learn more about these classes at www.MitchMeyerson.com.

Jay Conrad Levinson, the father of Guerrilla Marketing used the term *fusion marketing* to describe partnerships like these and others. It can be as simple as saying, "Hey, Jack, if you enclose my brochure in your next mailing, I'll enclose yours in mine," or "Emily, if you hang a sign for my business in your store, I'll do the same for you." If Jack and Emily are smart, they'll understand that they've just been offered great exposure for free.

Here are some examples of how online partners might work together:

- A copywriter teams up with a graphic designer and web developer to launch a dynamic web site that sells well-designed and useful information products to their combined list of prospects.

- One partner develops the curriculum, another provides the list of marketing prospects, and a third sets up, presents, and records a teleseminar series.

- One person researches and establishes the product lines, another develops the catalog descriptions and promotional content, and a third provides the technical infrastructure for merchant accounts and autoresponders for a web store.

As you can see, the possibilities are endless.

JOINT VENTURE PARTNERSHIPS

Joint ventures (JVs) are short-term partnerships based on a single project; they end when the project ends. Since each partner gets a snapshot of the other's work ethic, creativity, and follow-through, they provide a comfortable arena for testing a working relationship. And often, if the venture works well, they evolve into longer-term strategic alliances, where the partners work on multiple projects and continue to do so indefinitely.

Since they're generally temporary in nature, and one person can have many partners, online joint ventures work well when two or more people combine their skills and resources to create and market a single product, such as an e-book, CD series, or teleseminar. Here's how it might work for two people who want to develop and sell an e-book on a particular subject. Both agree to perform various duties, pay their share of development costs, and co-own the copy-

> **Synergy is the highest activity of life;** it creates new untapped alternatives; it values and exploits the mental, emotional, and psychological differences between people."
>
> —*Stephen Covey, author of* The Seven Habits of Highly Effective People

rights. However, once the book is developed, both are left to market the book independently and allowed to keep 100 percent of the profits they each generate. This is obviously just one of many types of joint venture arrangements. I prefer ones like this because they're fast, clean, and a simple way to leverage resources.

Approaching a Marketing Partner

Before choosing JV partners, make sure that you

- know exactly what they want most from the venture; it may not be what you assume

- are fully aware of your goals, and that you've communicated them to your would-be partner

- both feel that you can better achieve your objectives by working with each other.

While it is not always necessary, a good plan is to document the agreement in writing and make sure both parties review and accept it. The following are some quick tips for developing healthy joint venture partnerships:

Partner for a Cause

Don't overlook the value of cause-marketing partnerships; that is, give back to others by teaming up with a nonprofit organization to reach motivated niche markets. Today these partnerships are everywhere, from Robert Kiosaki's fund drives for PBS to Bono's Product Red line, which benefits AIDS relief.

And it isn't all about charity. Marketing studies are revealing that there's big money to be made through the hearts of American consumers. A 2002 marketing survey by Cone Inc. concluded that 84 percent of their respondents would switch to a brand that supports a cause. Similar marketing studies abound and savvy companies have put this information to good use. The IEG Sponsorship Report projected cause-marketing spending would rise 20.5 percent in 2007 to $1.34 billion.

Though there's real money to be made, the best cause marketing success is when your spirits soar to heights that money can't buy. To find out more and get help connecting with a cause, download free resources and the e-book, *Idealist Marketing*, by 20-year nonprofit veteran and entrepreneur Amy Belanger, at www.amybelanger.com.

- **Do your research ahead of time.** Make sure the possible partner is the type of person you like and that their business is healthy and respectable.

- **Approach them with a what's-in-it-for-them stance.** Don't concentrate on how great you are.

- **Be specific.** Don't leave things squishy regarding anything—this is how misunderstandings begin.

Go Platinum

We've all heard of the golden rule—treat people the way you would like to be treated. And while the concept is sound, it becomes problematic because it assumes that everyone has identical desires and perceptions. Authors Tony Alessandra and Michael J. O'Conner rephrased the tenet and renamed it the platinum rule. It goes like this: "Do unto others as they'd like done unto them." This requires a real understanding of others and what motivates them, and there's no better way of learning that than by asking them. Otherwise, we risk offending others by incorrectly presupposing the answer based on our own sensibilities.

- **Respect their time.** Let them know you value their time as much as your own.

- **Develop simple deals.** Try especially to create partnerships that don't require either of you to look over the other's shoulder.

- **Give before you get,** particularly if you're just starting out. People are understandably more leery of opening up their hard-earned business resources before you've proven yourself.

- **Avoid using a sales pitch.** That is no way to begin a give-and-take partnership.

- **Don't obsess over who's getting more out of the deal.** Make your best deal and forget about it.

STRATEGIC ALLIANCES

Once you've experienced a positive joint venture partnership with someone you'll probably want to consider taking on more. If your partner agrees, a strategic alliance—when two or more partners regularly work together on new and/or ongoing projects—is born. And although these types of partnerships have some of the benefits of more traditional, legal partnerships—stability, reliability, familiarity, and so on—they avoid their locked-in, static nature. In most instances either partner can, at any time, decline future jobs and adjust and amend the terms of a current project.

PART 2: AFFILIATE PROGRAMS

Sometimes referred to as associate or revenue sharing programs, affiliate programs are one of the most straightforward forms of online partnerships. Simply put, they are the internet's version of commission-based sales: people pay other people agreed-upon fees for selling their products or services. You can participate in an affiliate program in two ways: You sell other people's products and/or they sell yours. Very, very simple.

New online marketers can gain more visibility (sales and revenues) quickly by teaming up with more popular web site owners and established e-commerce businesses via affiliate programs. They are particularly useful for online marketers who want to offer their prospects and customers a wider selection of products and/or services but don't want to develop products on their own. Additionally, they're wonderful for companies that are looking to dramatically increase their sales. Think of it this way: You can build an infinite army of motivated salespeople, anywhere in the world, and manage it automatically.

> ## "People say New Yorkers can't get along.
>
> Not true. I saw two New Yorkers, complete strangers, sharing a cab. One guy took the tires and the radio; the other guy took the engine."
>
> —*David Letterman, host of "The Late Show"*

SELLING OTHER PEOPLES' PRODUCTS AND/OR SERVICES

Here are two basic approaches that work well if you're considering selling other people's products and/or services:

1. **Choose products related to your existing business.** If you already have an established e-commerce business, look for products and/or services that are natural extensions, supplements, or complements of yours. For example, a real estate agent targeting low- to middle-income consumers would do better selling do-it-yourself books and tapes on affordable renovations than pricey coffee-table books on architectural design.

Don't Put All Your Eggs in One Basket

As Robert Allen says in Chapter 2 of my book, *Success Secrets of the Online Marketing Superstars* (Chicago: Dearborn, 2005), the key to success on the internet is developing multiple streams of income. You need to have your web site generating revenue streams from all kinds of different avenues. It can't be just one; it has to be multiple streams of income because it makes your web site much more versatile. It also forces you to think like a businessperson. You start to think, "How can I squeeze the most amount of profit out of every single activity that I am doing on the internet?"

The other reason is—you never can tell when one of the streams of income that you are focusing on might be the big one; the big kahuna. It may be the one that is going to make you enormous amounts of money.

On the other side of the coin, you never can tell when one of the streams of income that you are focusing on might lose popularity for reasons you can't control. If you're focusing only on a few products, and one of them sees dramatic declines in sales, you're in trouble. Conversely, if you're selling a wide variety of related products—say four different online courses that you've created, each with related books and CDs, and interesting new technologies and services connected with them—and one of them sees a drop in sales, you're buffered and your overall income drop is less significant.

If you expand your offerings even further, by becoming an affiliate of several other online entrepreneurs whose products support yours, but don't necessarily compete, and you offer their books and CDs, new technologies and services, and a few nifty gift items to boot, then you're on your way to financial success through multiple streams of online revenue.

The list is obviously almost endless; just be careful not to take on so many that your site becomes cluttered and confusing. If so, you'll discourage repeat visitors.

2. **Create a new business.** If you do not have an existing web site or would like to venture out into new areas, consider developing a whole new online business with a particular theme. For instance, if you're a NASCAR fan, you might create an e-commerce site that offers only NASCAR-related affiliate products—T-shirts, models, hats, books, decals,

and so on. Basically all you would have to do is build a simple shopping-cart enabled web site, join appropriate affiliate programs, learn to promote your new site (often affiliates offer free training modules), and then you're ready!

HOW IS AN AFFILIATE PROGRAM MANAGED?

An affiliate program is usually supported by a database software program like EasyWebAutomation, which manages the entire system and

- identifies all affiliates (those selling the product)
- documents the appropriate commission percentage per sale
- monitors each affiliate's sales
- tracks each affiliate's preferred payment method.

All affiliates are assigned unique alphanumeric codes, which are embedded into web links and e-mailed to them. They can then add the links to any of their communication pieces—e-mails, articles, ads, and so forth. Whenever a recipient of the promotional content clicks on the affiliate link, it opens the product's promotional web page or shopping cart. If the visitor makes a purchase, the automated system documents and assigns the sale to the appropriate affiliate.

WHAT'S INVOLVED IN JOINING AFFILIATE PROGRAMS?

Here is a simple, step-by-step process for joining other web sites' affiliate programs after you've decided on the types of products you'd like to offer.

Step 1: Find Out if the Product Has an Affiliate Program

Go to the product's web site and look for words such as *affiliates, resellers, make money,* or *associates.* These are all indicators that the product has an affiliate program. For an example, look at the screenshot in Figure 10-1. Note the link "Make Money With Our Affiliate Program" located in the top of the box on the left-hand side of the page. Anyone interested in becoming an affiliate can click on the link and follow the simple instructions.

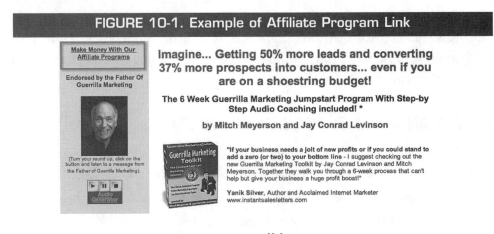

FIGURE 10-1. Example of Affiliate Program Link

Figure 10-2 shows another good example. This time the affiliate link is located on the top right-hand side of the page and says, "Make Money."

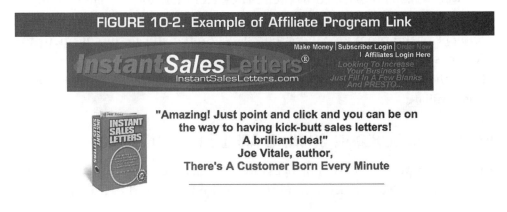

FIGURE 10-2. Example of Affiliate Program Link

Step 2: Click the Appropriate Link

In addition to finding out what's involved in signing up by clicking on the link, you'll get information on the company's commission payments, affiliate support programs, membership fees (if any), and more. Figure 10-3 shows my own affiliate page.

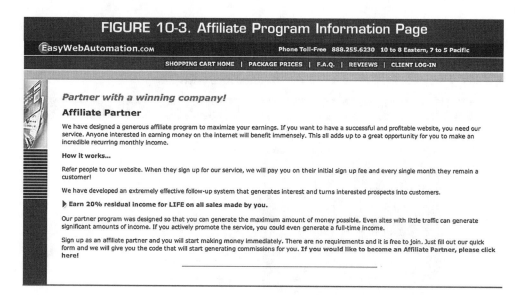

FIGURE 10-3. Affiliate Program Information Page

Step 3: Check Out the Program's Support

Make sure the affiliate programs you choose offer good incentives, and compare the percentages you earn with others. Additionally, verify that they utilize automated sales tracking (via unique codes) that is monitored by an independent company, and that your link will stay active indefinitely (vs. a 24-hour expiration date). You'll also want to see what types of additional services they provide such as marketing tips or training, graphics, and sales copy.

Step 4: Sign Up

Once you're satisfied with the commission and other details, sign up! Affiliate sign-up forms will vary, but they'll all gather the information needed to communicate with you and pay your commissions. For example, take a look at the sign-up form in Figure 10-4.

Step 5: Save and Use Your Affiliate Code

After you sign up, you should receive a welcome e-mail that contains your unique affiliate link and other information. Store this e-mail in a secure place on your hard drive; one that's easy to find. Then make sure you don't forget

FIGURE 10-4. Affiliate Signup Screenshot

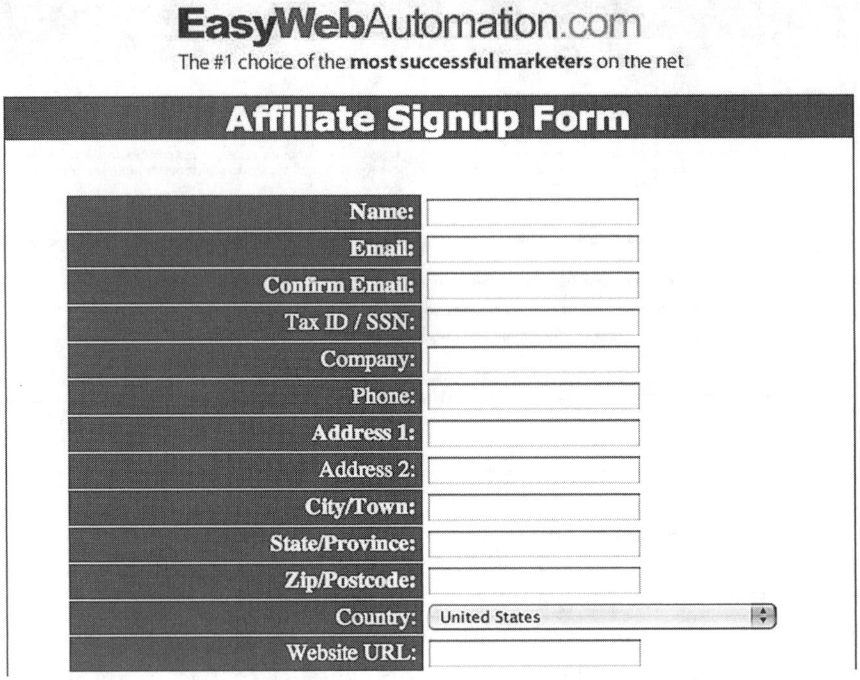

EasyWebAutomation.com
The #1 choice of the **most successful marketers** on the net

Affiliate Signup Form

Name:	
Email:	
Confirm Email:	
Tax ID / SSN:	
Company:	
Phone:	
Address 1:	
Address 2:	
City/Town:	
State/Province:	
Zip/Postcode:	
Country:	United States
Website URL:	

to embed the code into every affiliate promotion you send; otherwise, you can't get paid!

THINGS TO LOOK FOR WHEN CHOOSING AFFILIATE PRODUCTS AND PROGRAMS

Here are some quick tips for choosing affiliate products and programs:

- **Promote only products that you've tried and like.** Don't risk losing your credibility and reputation by aligning yourself with shoddy products, services, or companies.

- **Do your research.** Go online and look for products that your targeted prospects are already buying.

- **Choose affiliate partners who pay incentives quickly** and allow you to earn commissions on a continual monthly basis. For example, make sure you'll continue to receive a percentage for things like subscription and membership renewals.

- **Find programs that offer additional rewards for super affiliates.**

- **Look for affiliates that provide valuable marketing tools** and other resources (e.g., banner ads, articles, promotional e-mails, etc.).

- **Choose products related to something you love.** Let your passion shine through.

Now that you have a better understanding of how affiliate programs work and how to find partners, it's time to turn the tables and talk about ways to set up your own.

CREATING YOUR OWN AFFILIATE PROGRAM

In order to get others to sell your products and/or services, you'll have to set up processes for managing the program, recruiting affiliates, tracking sales, and making payments. Fortunately, there are several affordable ways to automate your affiliate program today. You can find out more at www.OnlineMarketing Superstore.com. Once you choose and purchase your affiliate management system, you'll be ready to recruit, pay, and reward your affiliates. Here are three simple steps for getting these tasks accomplished:

Step 1: Define Your Program

First, your affiliate program must be appealing to prospective partners, particularly to the high sellers known as super affiliates, and competitive with others in the marketplace. Therefore, you should offer them no less than what I advised you to look for in the previous section, "Things To Look For When Choosing Affiliate Products and Programs."

Step 2: Recruit Affiliates

Develop a process for recruiting new affiliates.

Here are some suggestions:

- Place an affiliate program sign-up link in a prominent location on your web site.

- Invite, via e-mail, current business contacts to become affiliates.

- Promote your affiliate program through existing business channels or partnerships, including e-zines, teleseminars, joint venture arrangements, and so on.

Step 3: Welcome and Support New Affiliates

Before launching your affiliate program, make sure you have the following prepared:

- **A welcome letter.** Make sure your new affiliates know how much they're valued.

- **Weekly or monthly update letters to affiliates.** Set up a sequential autoresponder to stay in touch with, support, and encourage your partners throughout the year.

- **Promotional graphics and images.** Include clear instructions for downloading and using them.

- **Marketing tips.** Don't make your affiliates reinvent the wheel or struggle unnecessarily.

- **Content samples and templates.** Create e-mails, articles, testimonials, and other promotional content your affiliates can use right away.

- **An affiliate support web page.** Include FAQs, contact information, and a forum for asking questions or posting comments.

Step 4: Reward Results

Since there are countless e-commerce businesses that offer affiliate programs, be prepared to compete for good partners. It's a great idea to make sure your incentives and system set you apart from the rest. For instance, you should

- notify and congratulate your affiliates when a sale has been made.

- make payouts in a consistent and timely manner

- reward high-achieving affiliates with larger commissions and/or free products.

- offer cool rewards, such as iPods or laptops, and contests that encourage healthy competition.

Step 5: Identify and Cultivate Super Affiliates

A few of your affiliates will stand out from the others. In addition to considering them for joint venture partnerships, you should also provide them with more personalized attention and mentoring.

Here are a few tips for cultivating super affiliates:

- Visit their web sites and sign up for their promotional materials for your products; you may gain valuable insights.

- Express your appreciation and encouragement regularly using personal notes and/or phone calls.

- Offer them free and/or discounted products or services; they're likely to return far more than you give.

- Send them a stellar testimonial that they can include on their web site.

- Create leadership and visibility opportunities for them; for example, free teleconferences, online chat rooms or forums, citations on your web site, e-books, and other marketing communication vehicles.

Creating profitable partnerships and strong affiliate programs will take time and persistence. However, they are vital components for mastering online marketing and achieving the rewards of an integrated and profit-producing e-commerce business.

WEB WORK: YOUR INTERACTIVE ADVENTURE

Now that you've learned all about affiliate programs, here are a few steps you can take to jump-start your income in this vital area of online marketing:

1. Do your research: Go to www.google.com and type in "affiliate programs." You'll find sites like www.affiliateprograms.com, www.affiliate scout.com,

and many others. Take some time and click on the links to discover as much as you can about the world of affiliate programs.

2. Go to www.clickbank.com and click on "Buy Products" to see what potential products you can resell. Also click on "Sell Products" to see how the affiliate selling process works.

3. After reviewing the tips in this chapter, approach five new JV partners, then add at least one new partner each week.

4. Explore setting up your own programs using affiliate software. Type "affiliate software" into a search engine to research various options, or check out my recommendations at www.OnlineMarketing Superstore.com.

CHAPTER 10 REMINDERS

Before moving on to Chapter 11, "Web 2.0: The Key to Using Social Media Effectively," let's take a minute to review the most important lessons learned from this chapter:

■ Today's internet culture encourages cooperation over competition and people power over going it alone.

■ Short-term joint venture partnerships are wonderful vehicles for testing a working relationship. Experience how the partnership feels and works before branching out into more long-term strategic alliances.

■ Don't overlook the power of affiliate programs—selling other peoples' products or having them sell yours. For many online marketers this can become the biggest revenue generator of all.

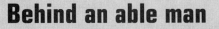

"**Behind an able man** there are always other able men."

—*Chinese proverb*

CHAPTER 11

WEB 2.0

The Key to Using Social Media Effectively

In this chapter you'll learn

- *what Web 2.0 is and isn't*

- *how to apply Web 2.0 tools and technology to strengthen your online business*

- *ways to successfully integrate Web 2.0 culture into your e-commerce web site*

...and much more.

"Change is the law of life.

And those who look only to the past or present are certain to miss the future."

—*John F. Kennedy, U.S. President*

Fueled by factors such as the proliferation of high-speed broadband connections, worldwide access to the internet, and an ever-growing reliance on mobile devices over desktop computers, today's internet users and online shoppers are savvier, smarter, and more demanding than ever. They are no longer satisfied with static, one-way, text conversations. They're tired of listening and are ready to speak. They are looking for content that's relevant, and don't want to slog through mounds of stuff to find it. They want instant, on-demand, and real-time information wherever they are, whenever they're ready, and with whatever device they're using.

> **Humans are producers**
> of their life circumstance not just products of them."
> —Albert Bandura, American psychologist and philosopher

So, if you're serious about growing and sustaining a thriving e-commerce business, you first need to understand and acknowledge this and then learn ways to use emerging state-of-the-art tools and strategies to stay one step ahead of your prospects and customers (and competition). And there's never been a better time to jump on the technological bandwagon that's been dubbed Web 2.0. Consider this: In 2006—and for the first time in history—*TIME* magazine's person of the year was not an individual at all. Rather the editors chose all of us—or "You"—and our participation in the new world wide web cultural and technological phenomenon known as Web 2.0. After considering several other notables, they selected this social revolution in which ordinary citizens use state-of-the-art internet technologies to share ideas (wise, wonderful, unpleasant, and appalling), expand social and professional networks, collaborate, and help and support each other for the award.

In my opinion, they correctly understood that this cultural awakening combined with powerful and easily accessed web-based tools affords all of us the opportunity to communicate internationally and materially transform the world —person by person. However, if you're like many online entrepreneurs, you may already be familiar with the term Web 2.0 but unclear on its precise meaning. While there are numerous magazine articles, blogs, discussion forums, web sites, and more devoted to the subject, its definition remains squishy, which increases the confusion, fuels debates, and keeps it a hot topic of conversation. That's why I chose to devote an entire chapter of this book to a discussion of this phenomenon and its importance to every online marketer's business.

And while space limitations prohibit a comprehensive and detailed exploration of this exhaustive subject (and there are many, many online resources available for those of you who want to delve deeper), I will provide a high-level overview of the essentials that will help you understand and embrace basic Web 2.0 tenets, and identify and apply valuable strategies and tools to grow your online business. But first, I'll begin with a few basics.

WHAT IS WEB 2.0?

Even though its name suggests otherwise, Web 2.0 is not a specific software or particular technology. The idea for Web 2.0 started during a brainstorming session between Tim O'Reilly (CFO O'Reilly Media, Inc.) and MediaLive International. O'Reilly vice president Dale Dougherty coined the term, which later became the name for a groundbreaking 2004 industry conference. Web innovators and pioneers were invited to share their ideas and experiences regarding the effects of the recent dot-com crash, explore the new opportunities made possible by innovative technologies, and help garner industry interest in the significant paradigm shift many were experiencing.

According to O'Reilly, most attendees agreed that the dot-com collapse of the late 1990s served as a catalyst for the Web 2.0 movement, then set about identifying, formulating, and communicating their ideas on what it meant.

Instead of a fixed, hard boundary, they described it as a universe of web sites that use some or all of the core practices and principles—processes, tools, technologies, attitudes, beliefs, and standards. In other words, it is an online movement that encourages users to participate in the fresh, interactive nature of the internet by using widely available, less expensive, and more mature state-of-the-art technologies.

For example, most of us are used to reading text (often referred to as read write) on a web page (although many web sites now use audio and video).

And even though many sites allow visitors to leave comments or ask questions, the conversation is essentially one-way.

The Web 2.0 philosophies challenge this paradigm and suggest that two-way dialogues (e.g., blogs, video logs, podcasts, etc.)—facilitated by the evolution of existing technology—are far more rewarding and satisfying. It demands that we think differently and move beyond the regular ways of communicating online.

> ## A journey of a thousand sites
> begins with a single click."
>
> —*Author Unknown*

You'll find one of the best examples of Web 2.0 at work on www.wikipedia.org—a site that allows anyone to add and/or edit its encyclopedia-like documents, and one of the first to encourage interaction, teamwork, and collaboration—core values of the Web 2.0 culture. Another frontrunner in the Web 2.0 movement is www.amazon.com, one of the first e-commerce retailers to promote visitor interaction by allowing users to leave comments, rate books and other products, and buy online.

And while this culture does make it easier to try new things, it does not mean that Web 2.0 is better than what's come before or that Web 1.0 is a thing of the past. Unlike computer software that is discarded when the latest version is installed, Web 2.0 is meant to enhance 1.0, not replace it.

BASIC WEB 2.0 PRINCIPLES

I believe that in order to explain Web 2.0 culture, it's helpful to highlight what makes it different than the older philosophies—we'll call them Web 1.0. Figure 11-1 is a simple chart that illustrates the differences.

SO WHAT DOES ALL THIS MEAN FOR ONLINE MARKETERS?

Bottom line: Things are going to change rapidly and, I believe, for the better. And although I go into most of these in more detail later in this chapter, following is a quick list of some of the many ways you can use Web 2.0 technology and its people-oriented culture to enhance your online business.

FIGURE 11-1. Differences Between Web 1.0 and Web 2.0

Web 1.0 Model	Web 2.0 Model
Primarily static, one-way communication; site owners talk, users listen	Interactive two-way conversations; users are treated as co-developers (e.g., Wikipedia, Amazon) and collective intelligence is valued (blogging, wiki sites, etc.)
Closed, proprietary networks and software, usually installed on the user's computer	Open source projects (e.g., www.sourceforge.net) using web-hosted software
Blockbuster mindset—big companies who use marketing dollars and branding to compete force-fed content by larger corporations with deep pockets	A more level playing field where the shared power of smaller, like-minded groups and sites is acknowledged and embraced using the long-tail philosophy
Desktop application software that requires down-loading, licenses, and scheduled update releases	Web is used as a platform and software is used as a service; open-access operating systems, applications, and utilities that continue to improve naturally over time—no upgrades, versions, or installations
Traditional marketing is main vehicle for increasing web site traffic and conversions	Viral marketing—recommendations from other users—is best method for improving traffic and conversions
Read-write text web pages, viewed on a single device, such as a desktop computer, and/or applications that can run only on a particular device	Flexible, mobile access (e.g., audio and video) that can take place anytime or anywhere on multiple mobile devices (e.g., cell phones, iPods, MP3 players, etc.) and open internet access to document-producing applications
Conventional one-way communication vehicles; web owners talk and their visitors listen	Social media and networking; enhanced communication software allows individuals and businesses to stay in touch, share friends and contacts, and expand social networks regardless of geographic boundaries (e.g., www.match.com, www.linkedin.com, www.myspace.com, www.rise.com)
Reliance on search engines to catalog, find, and extract links to relevant content	Collective intelligence is valued, allowing users to add consumer-friendly keyword tags to categorize (e.g., www.del.icio.us.com and www.flickr.com) information; add, delete, and alter web site text; and enhanced link structures for better search results

You can:

- **Get products to market faster.** Products can evolve through collaboration, user feedback, and time-saving tools and software (e.g., Google Maps and GMail).

- **Reduce risk.** Obtain fast, real-time data on prospects and customers, trends, and products that will help you make more informed decisions.

- **Build and maintain positive relationships.** Communicate more effectively, easily, and quickly with prospects, customers, vendors, and so on.

- **Change and add content, test offers, and copy and obtain relevant information.** Use RSS syndication feeds to help you stay informed, become more efficient, and conduct testing.

- **Engage in interactive conversations with the public.** Publish your own information using blogs, wikis, and tags.

- **Conduct real-time online video meetings.** Get the advantages of interacting face-to-face through a far more affordable and flexible process.

- **Monitor your word-of-mouth buzz.** Find out what others are saying about you, your company, and your products.

- **Use "mashups" to create, update, or bundle products.**

- **Attract more targeted traffic to your web site.** Use the "long tail" concept and readily accessible technologies to generate traffic.

- **Use tags.** Find less expensive and more effective keywords and put them to work for you.

- **Get information (and respond to it) the way you want.**

While I'm sure you'll agree that these are wonderful advantages, you may also be wondering if the technology is just too complicated (particularly if you have no idea what wikis or tags are) and/or expensive for novices. Rest easy and read on.

EFFECTIVE WEB 2.0 TOOLS

In this section, I'll introduce you to some of the most important (at least in my mind) Web 2.0 tools and show you ways you can use them to grow your e-commerce business. And although the language may sound strange and/or confusing, the concepts are rather simple and are really nothing more than cyberspace techniques for building teamwork, cooperation, and interaction. Even better, you'll able to use the majority of them for little, or no, money.

WIKIS: Helping Online Marketers Communicate More Effectively

Although a wiki is actually software that runs on a web server (so there is nothing to download), most people use the term to describe web sites where visitors can edit documents, articles, or pages. One of the key characteristics of wikis is that site owners do not accept authorship of their content but spread it out to visitors who can add, alter, and delete copy on a wide range of topics. Although they are as dynamic and interactive as blogs and forums, wikis are usually more encyclopedic and definitive in nature.

Flexibility is one of the best features of wiki software. For instance, they can be password protected to limit access for certain groups or individuals. And the system automatically retains all the drafts—old and new—of every document. That means users can view every iteration of a document, see when and how it was altered, and go back and grab previous versions. Again, there is no better example than the web's largest wiki site: www.wikipedia.org.

The main benefit of wikis lies in their ability to enhance communication, both internally and externally. Online marketers can add a wiki to their site to jumpstart conversations with their visitors by encouraging them to make changes to their content, add new information, provide feedback and opinions, and more. Additionally, they are wonderful tools for creating and updating instructional internal business content—policies and procedures, training, customer support, trouble-shooting, and more—in manuals, white papers, and other research documents.

You can get started using hosted software on sites such as www.pbwiki.com or with software you'll install on your site at www.MediaWiki.com.

WIDGETS: Helping Online Marketers Expand Their Reach

Widgets are small programs, scripts, or swatches of HTML that can be embedded into a web page. They allow online marketers to take advantage of the social networking aspects of Web 2.0 and offer a simple way for online marketers to appear credible without having to build these features into their sites themselves. Like viral marketing campaigns, widgets are wonderful tools for helping online businesses build communities of like-minded people within their web sites because they allow users to find content that interests them and pull it into their sites. Individual widgets can be grabbed by web visitors for use on their own sites with a link back to yours, and vice versa.

For instance, let's say you placed a widget on your site—an image with an embedded link that played the top ten songs in a certain musical genre. Any of your web site visitors could take that widget and place it on their site. Then when their visitors clicked the link, they would be directed back to your site, where they could play the songs.

Additionally, sites like www.widgetbox.com offer easy-to-use widgets that allow visitors to send text messages, combine news feeds, transport search elements to your site, and much more.

OPEN SOURCE SOFTWARE: Helping Online Marketers Tap Directly into Data Sources

New technology now makes it possible for anyone with an internet connection to share data and communicate through secure but interactive protocols using programming interfaces called Application Programming Interfaces, or APIs. A built-in collaboration feature allows you to download, import, export, share, and publish documents on the internet regardless of the type of software stored on your computer (e.g., Mac, Linksys, Microsoft Word) using any browser, because the documents and spreadsheets are embedded in the browser itself.

This open, ownerless system is united using a set of protocols and cooperation agreements and is the polar opposite of Microsoft's proprietary platform. Three great examples of these open network sites are www.joomla.com, www.OpenOffice.org, and www.moodle.com.

TAGS: Helping Online Marketers Publish and Search in New Ways

Very much like keywords, tags are tools for classifying search information on the internet, only they're far more flexible and open than traditional lists.

Here's how: Search engines organize web pages using rigid keyword categories (like books are cataloged in libraries) based on variables that they develop. This means that users receive search result lists based on the engines' predetermined criteria. Tagging, however, permits users to create and place their own freely chosen keywords on content they upload onto internet sites (ones that categorize using tags), making it another way for information to be found and aggregated. An easy way to see this in action is to log on to www.Flickr.com. This web site lets its visitors upload photos and tag them using keywords they choose —regardless of how many other people have used the same label.

So, for example, let's assume that John Smith uploaded photos of his recent trip to Costa Rica and tagged them "My Vacation." If he was the first to use these keywords, a new category named My Vacation would be created and his photos would be filed there. Alternatively, if he was one of many users who tagged their vacation pictures with "My Vacation," his would be lumped into the same category with everyone else. Either way, site visitors who searched for photos using the keywords "My Vacation" would receive links to John's photos, along with potentially thousands of others.

> ## " I think it's a good thing
>
> that there are bloggers out there watching very closely and holding people accountable. Everyone in the news should be able to hold up to that kind of scrutiny. I'm for as much transparency in the news-gathering process as possible."
>
> —*Anderson Cooper, American journalist and author*

As you can see, overly generic keyword tags such as these can make it very difficult to find explicit content. Conversely, it is much easier to find specific content when it's been tagged with more descriptive keywords; something that's harder for search engines to deliver using their constrained system. Here's a simple example of the difference: Let's say Mary Jones wants to sell a puppy. She uploads an ad and photo onto a web site and tags it: Brown and white, male, cocker spaniel puppy for sale. Then site visitors, who want information on puppies for sale, conduct a search on the site using all or some of the tagged keywords. The site's spiders identify the category established by the seller's tag and include it in the searchers' results list.

However, if the same people typed in these identical keywords in a search engine, the results list would contain only web sites that fit into their predetermined categories, which are generally much broader in nature.

Therefore, users might get links to sites for "puppies" or "white puppies" or "cocker spaniel rescue camps," or "male puppies for sale"… You get the idea.

So, how do tags benefit online markers? Simply put, they're wonderful tools for finding out what's going on in the marketplace and what people are saying about them, their company, and/or their products and services. For instance, www.technorati.com is a web site that sends out spiders—often referred to as meme trackers—that eavesdrop on blogs and gather information on today's hot topics, such as movies, news stories, books, fashion, and trends. Because they gather and report in real time, they provide a fast and accurate way to keep abreast of up-to-the-minute factors that may be affecting your targeted audience and help you stay one step ahead of the competition.

SYNDICATION FEEDS: Helping Online Marketers Receive and Add Content

Basically, *syndication* refers to communities of like-minded companies or people who promote and/or supply content—usually on a common topic—to multiple public broadcasting vehicles. Syndication feeds (e.g., RSS and ATOM)—distribution programs that allow anyone to obtain updates on their favorite web sites, news stories, discussions, FedEx deliveries, and more—have become one of the internet's mainstay tools. They make it possible for everyone with an internet connection to request information from any source and view it in the format they choose. It's very much like having your own research assistant who collects the most recent updates on information you specifically request, and presents them to you in one customized view.

And yes, in the old days you could go to web sites and select specific content, but it had to be fed from official news sources such as the *New York Times, Wall Street Journal,* and CNN. Nowadays, e-commerce businesses and news agencies regularly use RSS feeds to alert their visitors when something has changed—prices, articles, blog entries, and so forth—via an e-mail that briefly describes the content and contains a direct link to the information. They're wonderful tools for staying on top of today's hot topics, particularly as they pertain to your products and/or services.

For example, if you're looking for information on what's currently being discussed in certain blogs, web services such as www.BlogLines.com, www. NetVibes.com, and www.reader.google.com will send you up-to-the-minute information, saving you considerable time and effort.

In order to view the feed, however, you'll need a reader (also referred to as an aggregator), which is software that translates cyberspace coding into readable text. Although there are sites that sell readers, you can find plenty of free ones that work just fine (e.g., www.reader.google.com and www.newsgator.com). You can also create and subscribe to Google Alerts, which land in your e-mail inbox, avoiding the need for an RSS reader.

Once your reader is installed, you can subscribe to specific feeds in the same way you'd sign up for a newsletter or e-zine. Here's a simple way to do this:

1. Log on to your favorite web sites and look for the now-familiar RSS/ATOM feed icon (right).

2. Next, simply follow the site's directions for subscribing to the desired feeds. But remember, many sites have multiple feeds so you may have to sign up for each one individually or they may consolidate all their page feeds into one.

Additionally, online marketers can broaden their reach and enhance their visitors' experience by continually placing and updating relevant content or news on their web sites and adding their own RSS feeds. This is a great relationship-building tool because prospects and customers receive only information that they've specifically requested. And since feeds bypass spam filters, you can rest assured that the content will be received. You can even set up multiple feeds on a variety of subjects and track which topics generate the most interest among your targeted audience.

MASHUPS: Helping Online Marketers Develop New Products

Mashups make it easy for businesses to extract digital data from different formats and unite it to create one or more new products. In theory it is similar to the method Shakespeare used to craft his plays. That is, he combined stories, legends, and anecdotes from diverse sources and mashed them together to create an original comedy or drama. Today, wide open architecture allows software developers to grab information from a number of sources and use it creatively to build new products and/or strengthen existing ones.

One of the best examples of mashups in action is Google's collaboration with Craigslist (www.craigslist.com), an online community featuring classified ads. The two companies married their databases using APIs (Application Programming Interfaces), so buyers can now use Google maps to get maps or directions to specific neighborhoods on Craigslist.

The opportunities are endless. The best advice I can give you is to do some online research. Look around the web and see if your online business can be strengthened by joining up with others. Check out www.AuctionAds.com. It combines eBay feeds with affiliate management software so it can place ads directly onto web sites.

The Long-Tail Strategy and Tools

Today's online consumers have come to expect that they'll be able to find exactly what they want on the internet, no matter how unusual the request. For example, most consumers wouldn't expect their local used car dealerships to have their dream car—perhaps a vintage 1973 Mercedes 350SL convertible—for sale on their lots. However, they would expect to find one, or many, on the internet. That's why the world wide web is such a great place for uncovering small groups of hardcore fans—ones that traditional brick-and-mortar retailers ignore—and offering them the specialized products and/or services they want.

The problem is that most online marketers find this niching strategy to be a little scary at first, even though they may acknowledge that it's the best way to grow their business. Many fret over their ability to flush out these smaller segments and develop products that truly meet their desire for more specialized products and/or services.

Chris Anderson, editor in chief of *Wired* magazine, was the first to use the phrase "the long tail" to describe how this theory applied to the entertainment industry's ability to compete in the future. He claimed that because of almost unilateral broadband deployment and digital delivery (e.g., iTunes: there's no physical product to ship and an unlimited supply) media companies must target millions of niche markets if they want to survive. A great example of this is eBay—a merchandise warehouse with no warehouse— and another is Audio.com, a company that figured this out years ago. This hugely successful business inventories and sells an unlimited supply of electronic media—general and specialized—and never incurs the delays, costs, and risks associated with shipping, manufacturing, and warehousing!

In other words, media companies must shift their current blockbuster revenue model to a longer tail—one that strategizes ways to locate and mine smaller groups of like-minded people for their business. And while this idea of microsegmentation is not a new concept, Web 2.0 technology and culture have made it far easier for online marketers to find out who's really enthusiastic about very specific subjects—and then create products and/or services that truly meet their needs without dumbing them down or attempting to make them palatable for the masses.

Additionally, more and more smart online marketers are employing new business models that effectively use the joint power of smaller groups and/or sites to move their businesses forward. Once again, the internet juggernaut eBay is a great example of the long tail at work. Acting as a conduit, it lets small retailers and individuals sell one, or multiple, products and make it easy for them to take money. This simple, but brilliant, business model takes full advantage of the collective strength of previously overlooked segments.

What does this mean to online marketers?

1. Take full advantage of the long tail strategy and strive to become an expert in a very narrow field. The days of generalists are over, and there's little profit in trying to be everything to everybody.

2. Learn to use the following Web 2.0 tools to help you specialize:

- **Tags**: They'll help you find and attract more targeted traffic and buy cheaper, more specific pay-per-click keywords.

- **Wikis:** Use them to obtain instant feedback and suggestions from prospects and customers.

WHAT ELSE CAN YOU DO TO TAKE ADVANTAGE OF WEB 2.0?

1. **Mesh your business into the global internet.** In other words—socialize! Use Web 2.0 tools to interconnect your site with others. Take advantage of far-reaching sites such as www.del.icio.us.com to expand your network, increase your visibility and influence, and share your contacts with others.

2. **Make sure you're reachable.** Double-check to make sure that your target audience can find you—write articles, participate in forums and blogs, syndicate content, and so on.

3. **Stay on top of new technologies.** Web sites will come and go, but the technology will not. Make sure you proactively seek out information on the latest internet tools.

The summary chart in Figure 11-2 offers a quick reference of some of the most common Web 2.0 tools and how you can use them to stay one step ahead.

WEB WORK: YOUR INTERACTIVE ADVENTURE

Visit the following sites and see Web 2.0 technology, tools, and culture at work!

1. www.wikipedia.org

2. www.openoffice.org, www.joomla.com, and www.moodle.com

3. www.technorati.com and www.googleblog.com

4. www.craigslist.com

5. www.del.icio.us.com

6. www.newsgator.com

FIGURE 11-2. Overview of Web 2.0 Tools			
Technology and/or Tools	Example	Benefit	How Do You Get Started?
Syndication via RSS feeds	www.BlogLines.com	Users can program content and receive important updates.	Subscribe to an RSS feed. Add an RSS feed to your web site.
Blogs, wikis	www.del.icio.us.com www.Wikipedia.org www.Amazon.com	Web sites are more interactive and dynamic, and less proprietary. Users can publish and/or edit content.	Create a new blog or add to existing site. Participate in relevant blogs on other sites. Add wiki capability to your web site. Become a guest author on other blogs.
Audio or video that can be uploaded and viewed or heard on multiple devices (cell phones, digital cameras, iPods, etc.)	www.YouTube.com	Users can become media producers and interact with prospects in new ways.	Purchase a cell phone, or digital camera with a web cam. Subscribe to YouTube.com.
Interactive web conferencing software	www.EasyLive Conference.com	Allows for real time social interaction.	Purchase EasyLive Conference.com.
Tags	www.flickr.com	Find and store information in new ways.	

CHAPTER 11 REMINDERS

Before moving on to Chapter 12, "Momentum: The Key to Systematizing your Business and Building your Virtual Team," let's take a minute to review the most important lessons learned from this chapter:

■ Online consumers want real-time information about your products and services using multiple devices.

■ Web 2.0 is not a specific technology or software. It is a set of principles and practices.

> " **A very different philosophy** of management is arising. We are moving beyond strategy to purpose; beyond structure to process; and beyond systems to people...."
>
> —*Sumantra Ghoshal, management guru, economist, and educator*

■ Web 2.0 and Web 1.0 work simultaneously; one is not necessarily better than the other.

■ Online marketers can use Web 2.0 tools, such as wikis, tags, and mashups, to quickly and effectively communicate with their targeted audience.

MOMENTUM

The Key to Systematizing Your Business and Building Your Virtual Team

In this chapter you'll learn

- *ways to keep your online marketing momentum*

- *how to set up vital business systems*

- *why building your virtual team is so important to your online business*

...and much more.

> ## "Success is neither magical nor mysterious.
>
> Success is the natural consequence of consistently applying the basic fundamentals."
>
> —*Jim Rohn, author, motivational speaker, and business philosopher*

In the last 11 chapters you have learned how to create a strong business plan, write excellent copy, increase conversion, drive web site traffic, and more. And hopefully by now you have already benefited from the strategic and tactical advice you've received thus far. But it's really important that you don't rest on your laurels. If you remember, in Chapter 1 I discussed the number one reason that businesses fail—the elephant in the room. Now I would like to talk about the second elephant in the room: losing momentum.

> " **Business momentum happens** when you and everyone in your organization are moving in the same direction."
>
> —*David A. Scarborough, author, entrepreneur, and motivational speaker*

What do I mean by momentum? Simply put, you must continue to devote the energy necessary to keep the ball rolling. Think of it like a small snowball that grows steadily into a boulder on its way down a long, snowy hill. Your web site may be a snowball now, but if you maintain your drive and impetus, it will one day be that boulder. Therefore, you must continue to update and improve your products, service quality, and selection; web design and navigation; content and information; copywriting; automation; business and marketing acumen; relationships with prospects and customers; and a host of other things.

And although this may sound daunting, there are many things you can do to ease the way, such as:

■ overcoming the common challenges associated with maintaining momentum

■ building sound systems and processes for accomplishing tasks

■ developing supportive virtual teams.

In this chapter, I take each of these on separately and show you simple things you can do to keep your own snowball rolling down that hill!

PART 1: AVOIDING THE ROADBLOCKS THAT CAN SABOTAGE YOUR MOMENTUM

In his book *The 21 Irrefutable Laws of Leadership* (Nashville, TN: Thomas Nelson 2007), author John Maxwell calls momentum "the big mo." He adds that it is "a leader's best friend" and often the only quality that separates winners from losers. What Maxwell understands is that drive—that intangible quality that allows some of us to move around obstacles when others freeze—is a vital trait for getting beyond past mistakes and building multiple successes. While many people are energized during the early stages of a project, they lack the discipline and commitment necessary to sustain it after the newness wears off. And this is never more evident than on the internet.

People devote massive amounts of time and energy to creating new web sites, only to have them completely ignored once they're live. For example, some web site owners never create messages and schedule sequential autoresponders to prospects and customers, even though they know it's vitally important to stay in touch with them. They forget to reply to customer e-mails, decide that an e-zine is just too boring to write each month, or convince themselves that it's not important to regularly participate in online communities.

But if you apply the lessons you've learned in this book, you'll be thrilled with the result. Why? Because you'll have plowed through the obstacles and created a thriving online business. Even better, you'll have saved yourself time, stress, and money along the way; achieved your goals far faster than most; inspired a new energy that feeds on itself; built positive relationships; and most importantly, put yourself in a position to seize new opportunities.

But as I've said repeatedly, successful businesses—online or otherwise—do not happen in a snap. They are developed over time and only with consistent care. However, it's the ongoing work that many of us overlook.

So, what's standing in the way? Succinctly, there are many things that can sabotage your ability to keep your momentum going. For instance, you may be:

- **Overwhelmed**. Perhaps you're confused and not sure where to begin. You may be juggling two jobs and family commitments, feel paralyzed by financial burdens or stressed out over the amount of work you need to accomplish, or a host of other things

- **Distracted**. You're overcommitted, overstimulated, and/or going crazy trying to slog through the internet's massive clutter.

- **Bored**. Let's face it, the day-to-day realities of running and managing a successful business can be downright uninteresting.

- **Afraid**. You might be scared to begin and even more frightened when you think about failing.

In my mind, however, these are really symptoms of hidden deficits, and regardless of how they manifest themselves, we erect these momentum-draining obstacles because at the end of the day we lack one, or all, of the following three vital personality traits:

1. **Discipline**. This means honoring the promises you've made to yourself and others by regularly completing the actions and tasks necessary to achieve your goals—even when they're boring and mundane and you just don't feel like it. For example, you can set up one day a week to write and post new articles on your site and/or search for new ways to improve your daily processes.

2. **Focus**. This means paying attention to your most important goals and executing a well-thought-out, phased-in plan that works toward getting you there. Working hard on the wrong things is no better than not working at all on the right things; they'll both lead you to the same place— out of business.

3. **Commitment**. Keep your word. Do what you say you're going to do, long after the moment when you said it has passed. Adopt a long-term perspective and be willing to sacrifice short-term indulgences if foregoing them means you'll have an opportunity for a brighter future. Keep your eye on the finish line and take pleasure in the journey along the way.

If any of these roadblocks sound familiar, you may be wondering what you can do to avoid them and keep things on the right track. Following are some steps you can use to help you sustain your own forward motion.

ARTICULATE YOUR VISION, DEVELOP A PLAN, AND STICK TO IT.

If you're old enough to remember one of the world's current premier automakers, Toyota, during the 1950s and '60s, you'll immediately grasp the concept of creating a vision and never letting go. In those days, products labeled "Made in Japan" were overwhelmingly perceived as cheap—low price and very poor quality. So how was Toyota, a Japanese car manufacturer, able to completely reverse this stigma so that its products have become synonymous with excellence throughout the world—in just a few decades? The obvious answer is that the company improved many things about their products over the years, but at the heart of this lay three key elements:

1. a clear and motivating vision

2. a well-thought-out strategic and tactical business and marketing plan

3. stick-to-itiveness.

And the company's current tag line, "Moving Forward," is more than a catchy slogan for a car manufacturer. Rather, it suggests that Toyota's belief in, and adherence to, principles of Kaizen—searching for and implementing continual daily improvements, no matter how small—resulted in the company we know today.

> ## We are what we repeatedly do.
> Excellence, then, is not an act, but a habit."
> —*Aristotle, Greek philosopher*

So, if you dedicate yourself to the same tenet and look for ways to enhance your online business in tiny increments—even 1 percent daily—you'll have achieved a 365% improvement in one year! Talk about momentum! How does this look in the real world? Well, it can be as simple as:

- leaving 15 minutes at the end of each day to clear off your desk and write your to-do list for the next day

- sticking to a 24-hour deadline for answering all important business e-mails

- building a mini course by adding one new tip each week

- calling or writing one customer a day and expressing your sincere and personal thanks for their business.

PART 2: SYSTEMS AND ACCOUNTABILITY

Having worked with hundreds of online entrepreneurs over the years, I've observed that many of them have a tendency to reinvent the wheel every time they start a new project. They agonize over their ability to be really original and spend countless hours creating things from scratch. Not only is this a waste of precious time, but they risk creating something original that doesn't work!

For example, let's say that whenever your prospects, customers, or colleagues ask you to e-mail them information about one of your products or services, you compose a brand new e-mail. When you're small and focused, this might work OK for a while. But what happens when you've had a really long and frustrating day and the last thing you feel like doing is responding to another e-mail request? Well, if you're like most, you'll probably do either of the following:

- **Put it off.** You'll rationalize that you'll do a better job later and risk forgetting about it altogether.

- **Write and send a half-hearted, ill-conceived reply.** In an effort to get it done, it's likely that you'll omit key pieces of information, communicate a less-than-enthusiastic attitude, and/or ensure that you message is chock-full of typos and misspellings.

And these snafus are easily avoided. The very best solution is to automate! Set up autoresponders—letters that are created and automatically sent whenever a visitor requests information by clicking on a link. Alternatively, you can develop a boilerplated letter that you cut and paste into a new e-mail. If you use this method, you'll have to enter the recipient's e-mail address and name and send the message manually (which means you might still forget) but it's a better solution than starting fresh each time.

Regardless of the solution you choose, they each involve the creation of a *system* for accomplishing an objective. That is, you've broken down a task into a sequence of events and developed a process for completing it, just like a cake recipe! Obviously, there are as many systems as there are tasks. The important point to remember is that if you fail to build and use time-saving recipes for your business's ongoing duties, you won't be able to stay on top of those vitally important, albeit seemingly ordinary, obligations that will keep you moving forward!

Following are some simple steps you can follow to create a system for any activity:

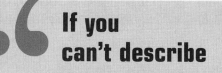

If you can't describe what you're doing as a process, you don't know what you're doing."

—*W. Edwards Deming, statisticion, author, and lecturer*

1. Identify the task you want to systemize and the results you wish to achieve.

2 Record all of the connected activities, steps, or actions involved in completing the task.

3 Depict this sequence of events in a precise, clear, and vivid format that can be shared, understood, and implemented by others.

A great problem-solving tool, and one you can use to help streamline your business functions, is called a *process map.* Since steps are graphically represented in order of occurrence, it is one of the simplest and most commonly used techniques for designing, analyzing, and illustrating processes. See Figure 12-1 for an example of one that author Mary Eule Scarborough (*The Procrastinator's Guide to Marketing: A Pain-Free Solution that Delivers a Profit-Producing Marketing Plan*) developed for answering e-mails. Also, unless you love to draw, I suggest you check into software programs that you can find on sites such as www.mindjet.com.

As they say, a picture is worth a thousand words. You'll be amazed at how much clearer things will be—you'll be able to quickly identify problems and communicate key steps to others—and how much more efficient you'll become. Once you have one system in place, it will be far easier to repeat the process for any task at any time. Even better, your new systems will help you

■ set benchmarking standards, whether yours or others

■ train others in record time—you and your trainees will have less trouble staying on track since you'll have a step-by-step process and they'll have handy reference materials

■ save lots of money and time

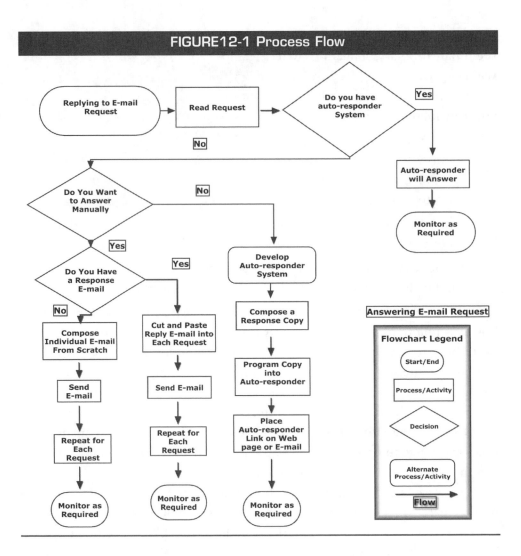

FIGURE12-1 Process Flow

■ stay focused—you'll be far less likely to become distracted since you'll know exactly what you're supposed to be doing, and when

■ relieve stress—you'll have less tension and brain clutter

■ avoid duplicating efforts—you won't have to reinvent the wheel each time you're faced with a similar task

and much more.

PART 3: BUILDING YOUR VIRTUAL TEAM

Online entrepreneurs often focus so completely on generating sales revenues that they often underestimate, and therefore ignore, the things they need to do to effectively and efficiently, such as following up with qualified leads and customer correspondence. As a result, prospect and customer inquiries or concerns may go unanswered, and entrepreneurs are perceived as unprofessional and, worse still, disinterested.

In addition to the direct consequences of customers asking for a refund, they risk losing profitable customers and/or gaining disparaging word-of-mouth assessments.

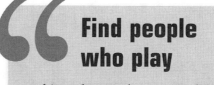

"Find people who play

at things that you have to work at."

—*John Assaraf, author, speaker, and entrepreneur*

So, along with creating internal systems to streamline your processes, you should also begin building your container for success— that plan that allows you to break away from some of the day-to-day routine tasks of your online business and delegate them to others.

And even though you may not be ready to relinquish the reins right now, you should develop your system for accomplishing this before you begin experiencing the inevitable breakdowns that come with increased business.

THE MERITS OF OUTSOURCING

Building and training teams of qualified people to help you is a wonderful way to leverage your time, because it allows you to focus your energies where they can achieve the most meaningful impact. And, in my opinion, one of the best ways to do this is by outsourcing work—hiring other people such as employees, bookkeepers, and contractors to work with you. Here's an illustrative example. Let's say Sally is a consultant who charges $250 an hour to advise and develop deliverables for her clients. Then let's assume that she regularly sets aside four full hours each week to generate and mail her client invoices, which means that she is unable to bill her hourly rate during that

Three Common Roadblocks

Melanie Benson Strick, founder of Entrepreneurs Success Coach (www.SuccessConnections.com) describes the three most common collapses entrepreneurs experience like this:

1. **The bright, shiny object syndrome.** This describes people who have are juggling too many golden opportunities and are trying to keep them all in the air at one time—possible investments, partnerships, new products, and so on. They chase all these bright, shiny objects, hoping that at least one of them will pay off and never develop a focused plan.

2. **The superhero syndrome.** This occurs when someone sets unrealistic goals. They falsely believe that they can do it all with the limited time, money, and energy they have. They don their tights and cape and are ready to leap tall buildings in a single bound, only they can't because they're not superman or woman and don't know how to fly. So, they get burned out and give up—the kiss of death for an online marketer.

3. **The multiple train syndrome.** Said more simply, this is the chief-cook-and-bottle-washer entrepreneur. They're their businesses' bookkeeper, salesperson, marketing strategist, shipper, operations manager, and more. If they don't come to work, the business shuts down—fast.

Each one of these is a role and the minute you take it on, it's like a train that is obligated to continue driving. And it works OK for a while; that is, until another train comes down the track and you have to hop off of one and onto the other. Pretty soon you're exhausted, overwhelmed, and frozen in place.

time (a total of $1,000). The way I see it, Sally's losing a lot more than a few hours. Since she could hire a part-time bookkeeper for $25 to $50 per hour, it's actually costing her $800 or $900 to do this work herself!

Keep this in mind as you continue to develop your online business and look for ways to delegate ongoing administrative duties and focus your energies on revenue-generating tasks or ones that play to your strengths and passions. That's why I pay an hourly fee to someone else who is trustworthy, reliable, and far more knowledgeable. It frees me up to write books like this one, advise clients, and market my online businesses.

Here are some professionals you can hire to help out:

1. **Bookkeeper**. If you're not good with numbers but want to keep your bank account under control, get someone to do your invoicing, reconciliations, and billing.

2. **Virtual Assistant.** This is someone who can help you with administrative duties or in many specific areas of your business. With all of the technology available today, your assistant can easily be located almost anywhere in the world. He or she can answer phone inquiries, manage e-mail, and schedule clients, among many other things. And as your business grows, you may even consider using your assistant as a kind of gatekeeper; someone who can provide people with appropriate information and shield you from routine calls that might take up large chunks of your time. I think a virtual assistant is a must for most online marketers.

> **"Perhaps the very best question**
> that you can memorize and repeat, over and over, is, what is the most valuable use of my time right now?"
> —*Brian Tracy, author and motivational speaker*

3. **Webmaster**. Unless you are somebody who really believes that the core revenue-generating activity in your business is developing and modifying web pages—which for some people, it is—then hire a webmaster, even if it is somebody who organizes, maintains, and updates content that you've already put in place. Even though you may be skilled in cyberspace technologies, maintaining your site may not be the best use of your time.

If you are ready to take the leap, here is a simple road map for getting started:

1. **Create a system for outsourcing.** Figure out what you want others to do, what they need to know, and what method you'll use to train them.

2. **Create a checklist.** Organize all the tasks they'll be responsible for performing.

3. **Practice an effective way to communicate with them.** Make sure you're prepared to provide them with the tools they need to succeed.

4. **Develop benchmarks for measuring their success and a system for tracking it.** That is, communicate very specific objectives and time-lines for completion and make sure they agree that the deadlines are realistic and doable.

5. **Test out your recruiting methods by hiring one person at a time.** Work out the bugs slowly, especially in the beginning.

6. **Streamline your hiring processes and learn to leverage.** Use templates, develop manuals, and record training sessions—you'll save time and money in the end.

HOW DO YOU FIND THE RIGHT PERSON?

Successful hiring starts with being clear about what you need: the specific tasks to be accomplished, and who you are (your standards, values, criteria, personality and your working style). Once you've identified these factors, look for people who can help you achieve your goals and ones who mirror your personality and style. You'll find that clear vision and/or mission statements are extremely useful tools for articulating your core philosophies and goals.

> **Managers are people who** never put off until tomorrow what they can get somebody else to do today."
>
> —*Unknown*

Then start spreading the word—ask for referrals from friends, relatives, and peers; place an ad on a site like www.craigslist.org; or go online and search for people looking for work. It all begins with the first step. For a comprehensive resource on building virtual teams visit www.MasteringVirtualTeams.com.

WEB WORK: YOUR INTERACTIVE ADVENTURE

1. List five distractions that block your momentum and find ways to manage them.

2. List five business activities you would like to systematize.

3. Make a list of all the players you want on your virtual team and begin the process of hiring them.

4. Get free up-to-the-minute blogs, advice, articles, and templates at www.MasteringOnlineMarketing.com.

CHAPTER 12 REMINDERS

Now that you're come this far, take a minute to review the most important lessons learned from this chapter.

- Don't rest on your laurels. You need to face the second elephant in the room: Keep the ball rolling and don't lose momentum!

- Successful online businesses do not happen overnight; they are built over time and nurtured consistently.

- You'll need commitment, discipline, and focus if you're going to become a thriving e-commerce businessperson.

- Along with creating internal systems to streamline your key business processes, consider outsourcing them to others.

"There is nothing so useless as...

doing efficiently that which should not be done at all."

—*Peter Drucker, author, management consultant, and professor*

AND CONTINUING ONLINE TRAINING

www.GMarketingCoach.com

Work With a Certified Guerrilla Marketing Coach or Become One

Get your own personal marketing coach to help you jumpstart your business or create a new income stream by becoming a Certified Guerrilla Marketing Coach.

www.StrategicMarketingAdvisors.com

Visit Mary Eule Scarborough's web site for great resources on online and offline marketing. Also check out her excellent book, *The Procrastinators Guide to Marketing*.

www.OnlineMarketingSuperstore.com

Our recommended resources for low cost domains, affordable and reliable web hosting and much more.

AUTOMATE YOUR MARKETING
AND TAKE MONEY ONLINE

If you want to work less hours and make more money, it is essential that you put your business on autopilot. The following are solutions we use every day and highly recommend.

www.EasyWebAutomation.com

Automate Your Internet Business and Take Money Online

Get a 30-day free trial and seven free *Million Dollar Online Marketing* audios just for visiting. This is the easiest and most effective e-commerce system on the internet.

www.EasyWebCards.com

Instantly Boost Your Offline Marketing with Online Technology

This excellent system will allow you to send personalized snail mail cards to your clients and prospects. This system provides a great solution for the growing challenges of email marketing.

MITCH MEYERSON has been a visionary, trainer, and author since his first book was featured on the Oprah Winfrey show in 1990. On the internet, he is the founder of three groundbreaking programs including the much-acclaimed Guerrilla Marketing Coaching Program, The 90 Day Product Factory, and Online Traffic School.

Mitch has personally trained and certified over 220 Guerrilla Marketing coaches worldwide and has provided consulting and coaching services to thousands of businesses, helping them grow their customer base and market share effectively and affordably.

Mitch is also the author or co-author of *Success Secrets of the Online Marketing Superstars, Guerrilla Marketing on the Frontlines, Guerrilla Marketing on the Internet, Mastering Online Marketing, When Is Enough Enough? Six Keys to Creating the Life You Desire,* and *When Parents Love Too Much.* His books have been translated into 25 different languages.

Mitch is a strategic thinker and is committed to achieving measurable results for himself and his clients. He is passionate about working with projects in the arts as he has been an accomplished musician for over 30 years. He lives in Scottsdale, Arizona. You can learn more about his companies and get free business building resources at www.MitchMeyerson.com

MARY EULE SCARBOROUGH, an unassailable marketing expert and thought leader, helps businesses of all sizes get and keep more profitable customers. A former Fortune 500 marketing executive, she is also the founder of two successful small businesses; an award-winning speaker; certified Guerrilla Marketing coach; and the co-author of the books *The Procrastinator's Guide to Marketing* (Entrepreneur Press), *Mastering Online Marketing,* and *Guerilla Marketing on the Internet*. She has a BA in Journalism/English from the University of Maryland and a master's degree in marketing from The Johns Hopkins University. Log onto her web site (www.StrategicMarketingAdvisors.com) for free marketing articles, tools, tips, and templates, or to learn more about her books and services.

As promised on our front cover...

YOUR FREE INTERNET TOOLKIT

($97.00 value)

Including:

Your very own online marketing mini-course
containing audios, videos and downloadable documents showing
you exactly how to build your own profit-producing
internet business.

As a purchaser of this book you will also receive
special bonus discounts
on our Mastering Online Marketing
and Guerrilla Marketing Online teleseminars
and special events.

TO GET YOURS NOW VISIT:

www.MasteringOnlineMarketing.com